Praise for *Why We Elect Narcissists and Sociopaths—And How We Can Stop!*

"Bill Eddy's newest book is a *must-read* for every citizen. The book offers a fresh, intellectually invigorating perspective on the endless political polarization and rapid rise of authoritarian leadership in America. Grounded in his concept of the high-conflict person (HCP), Eddy exquisitely expands our understanding of the dynamics of divided politics. He presents a well-researched historical view of how leaders (from both left and right) with authoritarian, high-conflict personalities have emerged as dictators in numerous countries worldwide. Eddy details a prescriptive, strategic action formula for preventing the predictable destructive outcomes of authoritarian leaders. This book will alarm you, inform you, and shake up your perspective—propelling you to take action—but only reasonable and effective action!"

—**Donald T. Saposnek, PhD, author of *Mediating Child Custody Disputes* and coauthor of *Splitting America***

"Understanding why people follow and support leaders with behaviours that are extreme and unwarranted is the topic of Bill Eddy's new book, *Why We Elect Narcissists and Sociopaths—And How We Can Stop!* In this fascinating work, the tumultuous and horrific impact of such leaders, how such individuals are shaped, and why they are supported are considered in the context of high-conflict personality and behaviours. Fundamentally, the book invites us to consider the role of 'Wannabe Kings' who have managed, often despite being considered incompetent or controllable, to be elevated to high positions and cause havoc. Importantly however, this book gives the readers, and those grappling with 'Wannabe Kings,' tools to prevent their ascension and to moderate the discourse that surrounds their grim reign. From the workplace to the political space, the book will inspire us to think differently about the tactics, behaviours, and personalities of some so-called leaders and revisit our approach to remake our future."

—**Professor Tania Sourdin, Dean and Head of School, Newcastle Law School**

"Thank you for this book. I wish I'd had it at the beginning of last year when I was running for Congress! A huge value of this book to me is to be better able to understand people trying to tear down our democracy. I learned several ways where I might have better persuaded erstwhile friends of mine to look objectively at candidates rather than following slogans."

—**Chuck Eddy, moderate Republican candidate, 2018 primary for Kentucky's 6th Congressional District**

"Personality disorders are dangerously important today, and it's vital we understand this better. We need this book."

—**Marjorie Kelly, author of *The Divine Right of Capital* and *Owning Our Future* and Executive Vice President, Democracy Collaborative**

"Author Bill Eddy has done a remarkable job of assessing the world of modern politics and those who have learned how to use their power to manipulate today's communication tools to influence unsuspecting voters. It is a brave new world. Bill has competently described the characteristics of many individuals who have no business in positions of power or authority but they are because they have learned how to work the system, to the detriment of the community, for their own personal advantage—a sinister scheme that plays out every day. Bill makes no distinction between partisan politicians, as his observations apply to many of those who seek power. As a long-standing member of the Republican Party and the chairman of the committee to recall the former mayor of San Diego, Bob Filner, I recognize that all of Filner's faults and failures can be directly attributed to the caustic characteristics so eloquently described by Bill. This book is a must-read for anyone interested in seeing how sausage is really made."

—Michael J. Pallamary, PLS

"The younger generations inherit an increasingly interconnected world, one with global problems that require international solutions. With such powerful world-altering positions being compromised, it is of great importance to know the warning signs and the proper response—else history will continue to repeat itself. In discussing top-ranking politicians that cause harm and controversy, Bill Eddy brings his expertise of psychology and advances a developing theory of high-conflict personalities."

—Crosby Doyle, recent graduate in political science and sustainability systems

"As a former judge and elected district attorney, I have dealt with several high-conflict politicians and elected officials with the characteristics that Bill Eddy describes in this book. He's right on when he says they create unnecessary crises and conflicts and see themselves as big heroes instead of doing their real jobs. His suggestions for what to do make a lot of sense for reasonable politicians as well as voters. This is a must-read for anyone running for or thinking of running for election and even more important for those trying to govern."

—Bonnie Dumanis, former judge and recently retired longtime San Diego County District Attorney

WHY WE ELECT
NARCISSISTS
AND SOCIOPATHS
AND HOW WE CAN STOP!

WHY WE ELECT
NARCISSISTS
ᴬⁿᴰ SOCIOPATHS
AND HOW WE CAN STOP!

BILL EDDY

BK

Berrett–Koehler Publishers, Inc.

Berrett-Koehler Publishers, Inc.
1333 Broadway, Suite 1000
Oakland, CA 94612-1921
Tel: (510) 817-2277
Fax: (510) 817-2278
www.bkconnection.com

ORDERING INFORMATION

Quantity sales. Special discounts are available on quantity purchases by corporations, associations, and others. For details, contact the "Special Sales Department" at the Berrett-Koehler address above.

Individual sales. Berrett-Koehler publications are available through most bookstores. They can also be ordered directly from Berrett-Koehler: Tel: (800) 929-2929; Fax: (802) 864-7626; www.bkconnection.com.

Orders for college textbook / course adoption use. Please contact Berrett-Koehler: Tel: (800) 929-2929; Fax: (802) 864-7626.

Distributed to the U.S. trade and internationally by Penguin Random House Publisher Services.

Berrett-Koehler and the BK logo are registered trademarks of Berrett-Koehler Publishers, Inc.

Printed in the United States of America

Berrett-Koehler books are printed on long-lasting acid-free paper. When it is available, we choose paper that has been manufactured by environmentally responsible processes. These may include using trees grown in sustainable forests, incorporating recycled paper, minimizing chlorine in bleaching, or recycling the energy produced at the paper mill.

Library of Congress Cataloging-in-Publication Data
  Names: Eddy, William A., author.
  Title: Why we elect narcissists and sociopaths : and how we can stop! / Bill
    Eddy.
  Description: First edition. | Oakland, CA : Berrett-Koehler Publishers, Inc.,
    2019. | Includes bibliographical references.
  Identifiers: LCCN 2019001488 | ISBN 9781523085279 (print hardcover)
  Subjects: LCSH: Political leadership—Psychological aspects. |
    Politicians—Psychology. | Heads of state—Psychology. |
    Voting—Psychological aspects. | Comparative government.
  Classification: LCC JC330.3 .E32 2019 | DDC 324.9—dc23
  LC record available at https://lccn.loc.gov/2019001488

First Edition
25 24 23 22 21 20 19   10 9 8 7 6 5 4 3 2 1

Book producer and text designer: Maureen Forys, Happenstance Type-O-Rama
Cover designer: Ian Koviak, The BookDesigners

To young voters everywhere:
May you avoid the mistakes of your elders.

CONTENTS

PREFACE

I learned about personality disorders, including narcissists and sociopaths, in 1980 while training to be a child and family counselor. It was an eye-opener. I didn't realize then that I would be teaching this information in regard to leadership and heads of state almost forty years later.

Understanding these disorders helped me deal with the most difficult clients I had, as well as a few people in my personal life. These people could seem reasonable and even charming on the surface, but they repeatedly got into conflicts with those around them that they expected me to solve. They didn't reflect on their parts in the problems and never changed their behaviors—even when they were the primary causes of the conflicts.

After a dozen years as a therapist, I decided to change professions to focus on conflict resolution and became a lawyer in 1992. I quickly realized that personality disorders were driving a lot of legal disputes, too—and in a bad direction. These disorders were not understood or even recognized by most legal professionals. Clients with such disorders had disputes that wouldn't settle; then their problems would grow and they would keep coming back to court. The uninformed professionals often made things worse.

I tried to explain to them that many people with personality disorders are stuck in a habit of blaming others, that they are always adversarial in their thinking, and that they often have unrestrained aggressive behavior. They need more limits, not more opportunities to blame others.

But lawyers said, "What are personality disorders? Forget about it, Bill. You're just saying that to win your case." Judges said, "I fail to see the relevance of this to legal disputes." Mental health professionals said, "Don't talk about those disorders in court. They will stigmatize people with personality disorders." These professionals didn't get it.

I found that I couldn't explain what was happening in five or ten minutes, so I eventually wrote a book about it that I completed in 2003. I couldn't find a publisher because they said there was no market for it, that no one would be interested in this subject. At the time, a friend who was learning how to set up websites made one for me. With the aid of this website, I was able to self-publish my book and sell it online.

Very quickly I saw that having a book and a website made a huge difference to getting my message out. I started to receive requests from around the country asking me to speak to groups of lawyers, judges, mediators, therapists, and others.

I taught them that high-conflict legal disputes don't just happen. They are *driven* by people with *high-conflict personalities* or *high-conflict people* (HCPs for short). Eventually I was contacted by human resource professionals, federal agencies, law enforcement, hospitals, universities, community groups, and city politicians who all wanted to understand the bizarre and unpredictable behavior of the difficult individuals who were draining their time, energy, and resources. I explained that their high-conflict behavior was quite predictable, once you recognized the warning signs, and it was simple to learn their patterns.

I started teaching my HCP Theory and developing methods for calming and resolving HCP disputes. After one of my trainings for judges, the organizer, Megan Hunter, suggested that we form a training partnership, which became the High Conflict Institute in 2008. The added visibility led to me speaking worldwide, mostly to professionals, but also to ordinary individuals struggling with HCPs in their lives. We soon augmented our services by adding a dozen trainers and online training.

Amazingly, the HCP pattern was the same everywhere. Were HCPs increasing, I wondered? The people on the receiving end of high-conflict behavior often tell us some variation of the following: "I wish I knew this years ago," "I can't believe they deceived me for so long," and "I had no idea how dangerous they could be."

It was around 2010 that political tensions seemed to erupt into high conflict. Increasing incivility between liberals and conservatives seemed to be occurring worldwide. Populism and authoritarian governments were sprouting all over. Could populist politicians be HCPs, I wondered? Many seemed to have these familiar personality patterns.

I began to wonder if it was possible to educate all voters about personality disorders and their destructive potential in politics. I realized I was having the same feeling as I did twenty-five years ago in the legal field. As I began to think about writing this book, I asked myself if people would say personalities are irrelevant to today's problems. Or that I was just taking sides, trying to help my favorite candidate win. Now that I have this written, I guess I'll find out. I don't mind if this book creates these controversies. I just want people to *think* about personality dynamics rather than simply react to them.

About This Book

This book emphasizes extreme cases, but the fundamental patterns herein can be applied to HCP leaders at all levels of government, business, and communities. I wrote this book in three sections.

Part I: How Narcissists and Sociopaths Get Elected

Part I first covers the patterns of high-conflict politicians, how their narcissistic and sociopathic traits can be extremely dangerous and extremely deceptive, and how you can spot them early on (Chapter 1). Next, I describe HCPs' *emotional warfare*: how they seduce and attack and then divide and dominate whole communities and nations (Chapter 2). This is made possible because voters tend to split into four groups that fight with each other endlessly in response to this emotional warfare: *Loving Loyalists, Riled-Up Resisters, Mild Moderates,* and *Disenchanted Dropouts* (Chapter 3).

I then cover how the *high-emotion media* attracts high-conflict politicians from the fringes of society and launches them into leadership positions around the world, multiplying their emotional warfare thousands of times to reach millions of people (Chapter 4). Finally, I explain how the core secret of their narcissistic and sociopathic power is repeatedly promoting stories about a *Fantasy Crisis Triad* ("there's a terrible crisis caused by an evil villain that requires a super hero to solve—me!") as the only way to sell themselves to voters, because of their lack of skills for solving real problems (Chapter 5).

Part II: The Fantasy Crisis Triad Worldwide

In Part II, I provide eleven examples of how Fantasy Crisis Triads have been used repeatedly by high-conflict politicians over the past hundred years to gain unlimited power. First, I analyze the original examples of Adolf Hitler, Josef Stalin, and Mao Zedong, including how their personalities developed and how they rose to power (Chapter 6). Then, I examine five present-day elected leaders from around the world who have taken their countries in a simplistic authoritarian direction using the same strategies (Chapter 7). I then delve into American examples that fit this pattern: Joseph McCarthy, Richard Nixon, and Donald Trump (Chapter 8). Finally, I review key mistakes that were commonly made in all of these examples (Chapter 9).

Part III: How to Stop High-Conflict Politicians

Part III looks at how to end this pattern of giving power to HCPs. First, I explain methods for building relationships among groups that have been divided (Chapter 10). Next, I discuss how to identify and explain the patterns of HCPs to the political parties who choose candidates, to those who campaign for them, and to individual voters who want to discuss this problem with other voters (Chapter 11). Then, I go on to explain how anyone can expose the Fantasy Crisis Triads of high-conflict politicians to others (Chapter 12). I address how to be as assertive as high-conflict politicians are aggressive to block their unrestrained aggressive behavior with a more compelling message that is presented *factually and repetitively* with positive emotions (Chapter 13). Lastly, I look at how individuals and news outlets can analyze fake news, to shift the focus from promoting HCPs, their emotional warfare and their fantasy crises, to presenting more useful information about real problems and real solutions (Chapter 14).

Conclusion and Appendices

The Conclusion reinforces the need to remain aware of HCPs in politics and the Appendices provide simple guides for recognizing their patterns and manipulations.

A Cautionary Note

The personality pattern information in this book may make you think of some people you know. *Please make sure that you don't tell them that you think they are an HCP or have a narcissistic or sociopathic personality.* This always makes things worse, whether you're right or not. Just keep this point of view to yourself and learn how you can adapt your own behavior to deal with them more effectively.

On the other hand, if you are talking with others about a public official or anyone who wants to be elected to a position of power, it can be very helpful to say that you believe the person may have a high-conflict personality. Then you can explain why this is such a big concern and describe the warning signs and patterns that you see.

Of course, you might wonder if you have some of these patterns of behavior yourself. This is normal when people are first exposed to high-conflict personality information. It's healthy to reflect on your own behavior (people with personality disorders don't do this) and consider changing it if you believe it is problematic (which they also don't do). If you continue to feel worried about anything you read in this book, I encourage you to talk about it with a counselor.

My Concern and My Hope

HCP politicians have the same patterns as HCPs in everyday life, but they have much more power to harm and deceive people on a much larger scale. That's why this is the most important book I have ever written. I want people to understand the seriousness of what we are all facing.

The greatest threat to humanity and democracy is narcissistic and sociopathic HCP politicians, regardless of their initial political identity (far left or far right). They are above and beyond politics and, because of their extreme personalities, they have been the cause of most of the world's suffering throughout history—especially the last hundred years—with no end in sight. As you will read, the conditions are as present today as they were in the past.

Yet I also have hope for three reasons:

1. We have had real success teaching tens of thousands of legal professionals about HCPs, how to spot them earlier, how to manage them, how to set limits on them, and how to help resolve their disputes.

2. For the last hundred years, as I describe in this book, HCP leaders have not had the support of the majority of their populations. Therefore, when the majority gets informed and organized, HCPs can be stopped—and this is what has happened throughout much of history.

3. HCP behavior has simple patterns that are easy to learn and teach to others. People like knowing and recognizing these predictable behaviors. When they do, they respond much more effectively and confidently in dealing with HCPs, rather than inadvertently escalating their dangerous behavior and making things worse for everyone.

You and Me

Throughout this book I speak of you, me, and us. This tends to be my writing style, but I also know from experience that we need to work together to deal with high-conflict people effectively. Imagine a world where we don't allow high-conflict leaders to gain power to create chaos and bloodshed and instead make room for reasonable leaders to join forces to solve real problems. We already know a lot about what works and what doesn't work with HCPs. We just need to spread this information much more widely. So let's get started. We may not have much time.

Part
I

HOW NARCISSISTS AND SOCIOPATHS GET ELECTED

Narcissists and sociopaths are the two most seductive and deceitful personalities on the planet. But most are focused on manipulating the people around them. The ones that go into politics can become extremely dangerous. They want to be on top—the very, very top—to be superior and to dominate others with an endless drive for more and more power. And yet their patterns of behavior are extremely predictable, including their inevitable and dramatic downfalls.

So how do they get elected? More specifically, why do *we* elect them? Yes, all of us. I will explain this in the five chapters of Part 1.

HIGH-CONFLICT POLITICIANS

I wrote this book to tell you about the personality patterns of high-conflict people (HCPs) when they become high-conflict politicians. Warning people about HCPs and how to deal with them has become my life's work. In this book, I want to tell you about how extremely dangerous they can be, how extremely deceitful (lying and conning) they can be, and how compulsively divisive they always are. Yet their personality patterns can be spotted early on, so you can avoid electing them in any setting and giving them power over your life.

Please note that this is *not* a book about politics. High-conflict politicians can be Republicans or Democrats or Libertarians, independents, liberals, or conservatives. They are mayors and governors and senators and heads of countries around the world. They are even elected to city councils, school boards, and homeowners' association boards.

They have *high-conflict personalities* because they have a *pattern* of increasing and prolonging conflicts, rather than managing or resolving them. They polarize communities, ruin the lives of thousands of people (sometimes millions), lay waste to shared resources, and go to war against their perceived enemies—verbally, legally, and sometimes violently.

A Worldwide Trend

This is also not a book that focuses on one particular politician, such as Donald Trump, even though he is a classic example of a high-conflict politician and he is included as one of the examples in this book. It's bigger than him. He's at the tip of the iceberg of a growing worldwide election trend that has picked up speed over the past thirty years and will continue to get worse until enough voters learn the warning signs of high-conflict politicians and how to stop them.

The Power of Personality

How serious a problem could one personality be? Let's look at what historians say:

> [The] wars and . . . megamurders of the 20th century can be attributed in part to the personalities of just three men.[1]

These three men were Adolf Hitler, Josef Stalin, and Mao Zedong. Hitler was responsible for at least fifty-five million deaths (by causing World War II as well as the holocaust), Stalin for twenty million, and Mao for at least forty million.[2] Were their wars, famines, and genocides inevitable, regardless of each leader's personality? Here's what other historians have said:

> But without Adolf Hitler, who was possessed of **a demonic personality**, a granite will, uncanny instincts, a cold ruthlessness, a remarkable intellect, a soaring imagination and—until toward the end, when, drunk with power and success, he overreached himself—an amazing capacity to size up people and situations, there almost certainly would never have been a Third Reich.
>
> "It is one of the great examples," as Friedrich Meinecke, the eminent German historian, said, "of the singular and incalculable **power of personality** in historical life."[3] (Emphasis added)

Other historians concur:

> As for World War II, the historian F. H. Hinsley wrote, "Historians are, rightly, nearly unanimous that . . . the causes of the Second World War were the personality and the aims of Adolf Hitler." Keegan agrees: **"Only one European really wanted war—Adolf Hitler."**[4] (Emphasis added)

Similar conclusions were made about Stalin and the genocide he caused in Russia and Ukraine through the forced collectivization of farms, which artificially created famines that lead to the deaths of over four million Ukrainians and more in Russia.[5] Even Stalin's wife committed suicide because she was apparently so distraught over her husband's ruthless policy.[6]

> There is no doubt that the collectivization drive was ordered by Moscow, imposed "from above," and that it was **Stalin's personal policy**, as first outlined on his trip to Siberia at the end of 1928.[7] (Emphasis added)

Likewise, Mao imposed a similar collectivization effort within China, which he called the Great Leap Forward.

> Impervious to signals from reality informing him that his Great Leap Forward was a great leap backward, Mao masterminded a famine that killed between 20 million and 30 million people.[8]

This and the Cultural Revolution had one source:

> As for China, it is inconceivable that the record-setting famine of the Great Leap Forward would have occurred but for **Mao's harebrained schemes** . . . . [T]he principal responsibility for the Cultural Revolution—a movement that affected tens of millions of Chinese—rests with one man. **Without Mao, there could not have been a Cultural Revolution.**[9] (Emphasis added)

The Causes of Political Conflict

You may wonder, as I did, aren't political problems mostly caused by simmering historical disputes? Or racial and ethnic hatreds? Or economic troubles? The answer to each of these questions? Much less than you would expect.

For example, in Africa, from 1960 to 1979, when so many former colonies gained their independence from their European conquerors, at least 160 ethnic groups were living side by side with the potential for violence between them: riots, civil wars, genocide. Yet violence broke out in less than 1 percent of them.

After the Soviet Union broke up at the end of the 1980s, 45 ethnic groups had the potential to break out into armed conflicts. Yet historians found that only 4.4 percent of these potential ethnic hatreds burst into warfare.[10]

The Yugoslav Wars of the 1990s, when Yugoslavia broke up into smaller countries with the collapse of the Soviet Union, were unusual for one reason: they involved the apparent high-conflict personalities of a few key leaders, who escalated prior co-existence into genocidal violence and who were later tried for war crimes by the International Criminal Tribunal for the former Yugoslavia.[11] Without these likely HCP leaders, would these wars have occurred at all?

Perhaps you wonder if these were unusual circumstances in which an HCP politician was like a match on gasoline that was already poured—that these countries were already highly dysfunctional. For example, weren't the economic problems of Germany after World War I and the global stock market crash the driving forces in the rise of Hitler? Not exactly. Here's how an American reporter stationed in Germany described the typical Nazi in 1932 when Hitler was gaining power:

> He was male, in his early thirties, a town resident of lower middle-class origin, without high school education; . . . had no political affiliations before joining the National Socialist [Nazi] party and belonged to no veteran or semi-military organizations. . . . He was strongly dissatisfied with the republican regime in Germany, but had **no specific anti-Semitic bias**. His **economic status was secure**, for not once did he have to change his occupation, job, or residence, nor was he ever unemployed."[12] (Emphasis added)

So poverty itself doesn't necessarily drive political conflict, either. Apparently, Hitler didn't get his followers from the poorest people—or the most prejudiced. Even though anti-Semitism existed for centuries throughout Europe, Hitler *taught* the German people to hate Jews at a level they never had before. As the cultural leader of the nation, he was able to directly condition the German people to his way of thinking, primarily through his radio speeches, which reached into many Germans' homes, and movies of his rallies, which dominated the theaters—"playing on their fears, resentments and prejudices more masterfully than anyone else."[13]

Three Key Questions

As I researched political conflicts—large and small—for this book, three key questions about the power of personality emerged that are relevant to today's events:

1. Can one high-conflict politician turn a well-functioning community— or nation—into one that is extremely polarized? If so, how does this occur?

2. In a time of peace, can one high-conflict politician lead a nation into war, famine, and genocide? If so, how does this occur?

3. Can we stop high-conflict politicians before they get this far?

In researching and writing this book, I have attempted to answer these questions. To understand the answers, we first need to look more closely at the personality patterns of HCPs, narcissists, and sociopaths and how they think differently about conflict from everyone else—and what happens when these three personalities combine in one person.

What Is a High-Conflict Personality?

Our individual *personality* is how we regularly think, feel, and act. When most of us find ourselves in a dispute, our natural inclination is to attempt to resolve it. But for someone with a high-conflict personality, as I have repeatedly observed in hundreds of disputes, the opposite is true. They *think* all relationships are inherently adversarial; they constantly *feel* threatened as an adversary (even when they're not); and they often *react* in an extremely adversarial manner.

As a result, in almost any situation, they tend to create one unnecessary conflict after another because they *think* conflicts already exist all around them. They *feel* at war with the world and project this feeling onto others.

Worse, they have no interest in resolving conflicts. Instead, they usually make them worse—no matter how many other people get hurt and no matter how much their actions end up hurting themselves.

People with high-conflict personalities are intensely driven (although usually unconsciously) to control, remove, or destroy their perceived enemies. They ultimately sabotage themselves, but they can't see it coming.

Although each high-conflict person is unique, all HCPs share a narrow pattern of behavior that includes four key characteristics:

THE HIGH-CONFLICT PERSONALITY PATTERN

1. A preoccupation with blaming others: their *Targets of Blame*

2. All-or-nothing thinking and solutions

3. Unmanaged or intense emotions

4. Extreme negative behaviors that 90 percent of people would never do

HCPs also have traits of one or more personality disorders. Personality disorders have been a hidden mental illness that most people have not heard about until recent years, because people afflicted with them can appear to function well some of the time. But they are: 1) impaired in their relationships, 2) don't reflect on their own behavior, and 3) don't change. These three characteristics can make people with personality disorders very difficult to be around, sooner or later.

Although research has suggested that those with personality disorders are about 15 percent of the adult population,[14] I believe that HCPs are only about 10 percent of the adult population. Not all people with personality disorders are preoccupied with Targets of Blame, and not all HCPs have personality disorders—but they all have some traits of personality disorders such as narcissistic or sociopathic.

HCPs compulsively act in self-defeating ways over and over again. That's why they stay in conflict, because they don't try to change or improve anything about themselves even when they are the conflict's primary or only cause.

They lack insight into their own high-conflict behavior, so when things go badly, they get more and more defensive and attack those around them: their *Targets of Blame.*

For this reason, they often have no real friends and develop a bad reputation in their communities. They are your lousy neighbors who may physically threaten you or make your life stressful with their endless complaints. They are your most difficult co-workers, bosses, and business owners. And, of course, they can also be family members.

HCPs are everywhere, but most people just think they're jerks—isolated, angry, poorly adjusted individuals. They don't see the pattern. They don't realize that HCPs are at the center of so many of today's problems and that there are so many of them.

They have a presence in every country and in every culture. HCPs are not an American problem, or a Western problem: they are a human problem—one that appears to be increasing, year by year. Unless you live alone in the wilderness, you cannot avoid them.

Extreme Charm and Persuasion

Another surprising and notable aspect of HCPs enables them to often get what they want. They can be extremely charming, persuasive, and charismatic. At least, that's how they show themselves to others at first. Then, when they get close to people or conflicts arise, their façade crumbles and they start to show their true colors. If you want to see how predictable HCPs are, refer to Appendix A: 40 Predictable Behaviors of HCPs.

CAUTIONARY NOTE: DON'T LABEL PRIVATE PEOPLE

By now you probably can think of a few people that fit this pattern. If you can, *don't tell them you think they are HCPs!* If they have this pattern (and most of us know someone we suspect has this problem), they will hate or resent you for saying as much, and they'll probably make you their next Target of Blame.

Let me emphasize that HCPs do not choose to be difficult. All personalities are the result of three basic factors, none of which we have control over while growing up. It's hard to know which played a bigger part in any one person's development, but it's usually a combination:

Genetic tendencies at birth. These may be part of the human personality gene pool because certain traits have been helpful over time, such as high-conflict traits during times of war.

Early childhood experiences. These can include child abuse or even indulgence. Loss of a parent, separation from a parent or insecure attachment to a parent at an early age can have devastating effects.

Cultural environment. Some say that the decade you're born in shapes your personality as much as your family. Over the last few decades, the focus on the individual, electronic devices and the excessive focus on self-esteem have all contributed to an increase in the culture of narcissism.[15]

This means that we should have compassion for HCPs, but at the same time we need to set firm limits to protect ourselves from their behavior.

The key is to adapt your own behavior rather than to try to change theirs. Avoid trying to give them insight into themselves or endlessly discussing the past. Just focus on what to do now, such as focusing on your own choices going forward. And don't choose them to be your partner, your team leader, your boss, or your local (or national) leader.

Why Are There So Many HCPs in Politics Today?

I can think of at least two reasons for this:

1. HCPs can be mayors, governors, or even presidents. But some high-conflict people really want to be kings (or, sometimes, queens). HCPs are profoundly attracted to the glory and attention, vindication and validation of being elected—and to gaining, having, and exercising absolute power. In particular, they relish having the power to publicly blame, punish, or destroy anyone they view as their enemy. They love the fight—the adversarial process. But, above all, they want to *win* and they want to *dominate*—and they want everyone to *know* that they won, and to see them as the absolute top of the heap.

   They want to be the strongman. The person no one challenges. The person everybody loves—or at least obeys or bows down to. The person with the power and the glory. And they are driven to do every-thing they can to make this happen, regardless of the consequences to others or even to themselves. They have *unrestrained aggressive behavior*. They are fundamentally authoritarian, because it's all about them and their unlimited power over everyone else.

2. They are particularly drawn to the fantasy world of today's *high-emotion media*. In their various forms (network and cable TV, Face-book, YouTube, etc.), these platforms do not require politicians to have any leadership experience or political skill in order to provide them with lots of attention. In fact, acting badly gets them more attention than leadership skills do. Those HCPs who lack empathy and remorse are good at creating fantasy images of themselves with no regard for the truth—the charming storytellers who emotionally grab the voters who are already primed for tales of crises, heroes, and villains.

   Plus, high-emotion media *craves* high-conflict personalities. They have the most exciting, dramatic, and expressive faces and voices that work particularly well on screens and speakers, large and small—and they sell the most advertising. With their emotional intensity, all-or-nothing thinking, and seemingly unpredictable extreme behavior, they are natural performers. High-emotion media attracts HCPs like basketball attracts tall players. They are the best in the game.

But which HCPs are attracted to politics? There are five types of HCPs: narcissistic, antisocial, borderline, paranoid, and histrionic. (See my book *5 Types of People Who Can Ruin Your Life* for more on all five.) But most aren't interested in being in charge of a community or nation. The two most charming, deceptive, and dangerous leaders are the HCPs with traits of narcissistic and sociopathic personality disorders. Occasionally we see traits of the others as well, but mostly these are the two personalities that seek to be leaders.

Personality Disorders

I'm sure you have met some narcissists and sociopaths. They are everywhere. In their extreme form, these are two of the ten personality disorders in the diagnostic manual of the American Psychiatric Association, known as the *Diagnostic and Statistical Manual of Mental Disorders, Fifth Edition* (DSM-5).[16] But I will not be determining whether the HCPs we discuss have these disorders. Instead, my goal is to describe the conflict behavior patterns of these personalities so that you can spot them when you are getting ready to make voting decisions. The issue of whether HCPs simply have some traits of these personalities or full-blown personality disorders is less important—either case is a problem when we are choosing leaders.

Generally people with narcissistic personalities are self-absorbed, feel entitled to special treatment, have grandiose ideas, have fantasies of unlimited success and power, lack empathy, and are driven to show that they are superior to others. People with sociopathic personalities (also known as *antisocial* personalities) frequently violate rules and laws, are routinely deceptive (lying and conning), are highly aggressive, lack remorse, and are driven to dominate others.

However, not all people with one of these personalities are HCPs, because some don't focus on *Targets of Blame*. And many of them have no interest in politics. But the ones who are interested in politics and know how to focus their attention (and the attention of others) on their *Targets of Blame* are the most dangerous. They are the ones who *want* to get elected and are driven to be in charge to dominate their targets. Let's look at each of these types of personality, separately at first, and then let's see what happens when they are combined into one person.

Narcissistic Personality Traits

Narcissists are preoccupied with looking and being superior to others. Narcissistic HCPs make demeaning statements—often in public—against their Targets of Blame, including their spouses, their children, co-workers, neighbors, bosses, or heads of organizations. In order to appear superior, they must put other people down. They do this a lot.

This characteristic makes politics appealing to them: political races provide them with opportunities to show that they are better than everyone else. They can *win*. And in the process, they can get revenge on anyone who tries to expose that they are not superior to everyone else.

Yet HCPs generally don't have the flexible political skills they need for the jobs they are running for, so instead they divert attention and keep the focus on their Targets of Blame. They persuade everyone else that they are better than *that* terrible candidate. But they also have grandiose ideas. They often convince others that these ideas can come true, but only if they are made leader.

The most narcissistic HCPs are attracted to the highest offices, because that proves that they are the *most superior*. Winning such an office also gives them the power to really demean everyone else, especially their targets.

Diagnosing any personality disorder is generally very subjective and based on the information available. Even experienced mental health professionals often disagree. This is fine for our purposes, because we're not trying to reach a diagnosis here. We're just trying to recognize *high-conflict behavior patterns* that may cause a person to be dangerous and deceptive and therefore not someone who should be elected.

Narcissistic personality disorder (NPD) is an extreme form of narcissism. According to the DSM-5, someone with NPD has internal distress and/or social impairment,[17] and exhibits at least five out of nine specific characteristics.[18] For the purposes of this book (since we're not diagnosing disorders but understanding high-conflict behavior patterns), the key narcissistic traits to look for are these:

KEY HIGH-CONFLICT BEHAVIORS OF NARCISSISTS

1. Drive to be superior

2. Grandiose ideas

3. Fantasies of unlimited power

4. Lack of empathy

These four characteristics help narcissists get elected because they help the candidates convince people that they *are* really superior and that their grandiose ideas *are* really achievable. Since narcissists truly believe in themselves and their ideas, they can appear very charming, authentic, and persuasive. But they tend to deceive everyone, including themselves. Although they aren't necessarily lying, they are usually unaware of how exaggerated and unrealistic they are about their own abilities and ideas.

For example, studies have shown that when narcissists are CEOs of companies, their preoccupation with themselves and their overestimation of their own skills creates more volatility for the company's performance. They are not popular bosses, are seen as below average in leadership skills, and take credit for other's work. They are usually not very successful when compared to CEO's who put the organization first.[19]

A large study determined that about 6.2 percent of the United States population has NPD. That's about twenty million people. This study found that just over 60 percent of the people with this disorder are male and just under 40 percent are female.[20]

Sociopathic (Antisocial) Personality Disorder

The DSM-5 lists several characteristics for *antisocial personality disorder* (*antisocial* is an equivalent term for *sociopath*), or *ASPD*.[21] For the purposes of spotting sociopathic high-conflict behavior patterns, look out for the following four traits:

KEY HIGH-CONFLICT BEHAVIORS OF SOCIOPATHS

1. Drive to dominate

2. Deceitful (lying and conning)

3. Highly aggressive

4. Lack of remorse

Research indicates that nearly 4 percent of the population has ASPD. That's over twelve million people in the United States alone. About 75 percent of them are male and about 25 percent are female.[22]

Sociopathic HCPs naturally gravitate toward positions in which they can dominate and humiliate others—such as politics, business, organizational leadership, and/or criminality. They may become CEOs of large corporations, politicians, and highly paid consultants; or gang leaders, heads of drug cartels, and leaders of terrorist groups.[23] A sociopathic HCP can also be a common criminal; a smiling, friendly, drug-dealing neighbor; or a heartless co-worker. You don't want to become their target by getting too close to them, joining in any of their schemes, or directly confronting them by yourself.

Some sociopathic HCPs are attracted to politics because they can steal from the public coffers for themselves and/or engage in large-scale schemes of swindling others. They enjoy that kind of dominance and high risk taking. They can also use their political power to boss around large groups of people by fooling them, controlling them, removing them, or destroying them.

They use Targets of Blame as a distraction while they are doing their dirty work. By getting you to look over there at another politician, they are able to take power and whatever else they want without being stopped. It's just like pickpockets who distract you by bumping into you and pointing somewhere else: "Look up at that over there!" they shout, grabbing your wallet while you're looking up.

You might wonder what the difference is between narcissistic and sociopathic personalities. Here's what the DSM-5 says: "[N]arcissistic personality disorder does not include characteristics of impulsivity, aggression, and deceit."[24] So if a politician seems narcissistic, but also lies a lot and is highly impulsive and aggressive, that probably means that he (or she) has traits of both disorders.

Malignant Narcissism

Now it gets really frightening. If someone has both of these personality disorders, they are considered to be a *malignant narcissist*, which is a disorder that experts say has "no treatment and no cure."[25]

The malignant narcissist can be particularly powerful, persuasive, confident, and aggressive. They can look very attractive and charismatic while promoting extremely grandiose plans (their narcissistic side). They are ruthless, heartless, and lack a conscience (their antisocial side). They are also paranoid and sadistic,[26] say the experts, so they are more driven than most narcissists or sociopaths to destroy their Targets of Blame—including almost everything and everyone in their path—and, ultimately, themselves.

This diagnosis was identified by German-born psychiatrist Erich Fromm who left Nazi Germany in the 1930s and came to the United States where he had a significant influence on the development of psychological theory and practice. Here's how Fromm explained this particular disorder:

> The Egyptian Pharoahs, the Roman Caesars, the Borgias, Hitler, Stalin, Trujillo—they all show certain similar features. They have attained absolute power; their word is the ultimate judgment of everything, including life and death; there seems to be no limit to their capacity to do what they want. . . .
>
> It is a madness that tends to grow in the lifetime of the afflicted person. The more he tries to be god, the more he isolates himself from the human race; this isolation makes him more frightened, everybody becomes his enemy, and in order to stand the resulting fright he has to increase his power, his ruthlessness, and his narcissism.[27]

Fromm says that this narcissism is *malignant* because it is not restrained in its growth, like a malignant cancer.[28]

The major study of personality disorders mentioned previously indicated that approximately 0.7 percent of the United States population has both of these disorders.[29] Although that sounds small, it's about two million people. They can be in any walk of life, at any level of society.

For example, Brian David Mitchell, the kidnapper of fourteen-year-old Elizabeth Smart from her home in Utah in 2002, was identified as having both narcissistic and antisocial personality disorders during his criminal trial. He apparently wanted to rule a family with many wives and had plans to kidnap more teenage girls because he believed they would be easier to mold to his wishes. He couldn't stop himself. Fortunately he was captured, and Elizabeth Smart is doing well and is educating the public about how such dangerous personalities can exist *anywhere*.[30]

Conclusion

In short, narcissists, sociopaths, or both, when combined with high-conflict personalities, are driven to be the kings (or, to a much lesser extent, queens), the dictators, the supreme ruler over all. I think of them as *HCP Wannabe Kings*. And these aren't the friendly Camelot or Disney type of kings. These are the grandiose and ruthless Wannabe Kings who will do anything and destroy anyone to gain power to become the absolute ruler.

Now you have the fundamentals for identifying the *patterns* of high-conflict politicians, including the narcissists, the sociopaths (antisocial), and the combination (malignant narcissists). Figure 1 is a simple way to summarize their characteristics.

Throughout the rest of this book, I refer to this personality pattern as HCP Wannabe Kings, HCP politicians, or simply HCPs or Wannabe Kings. Consider these terms as equivalent in describing this set of characteristics.

This pattern awareness gives you the ability to predict much of an HCP's future behavior early on, unlike most people who simply look at each of their actions in isolation and constantly express surprise. With practice, you

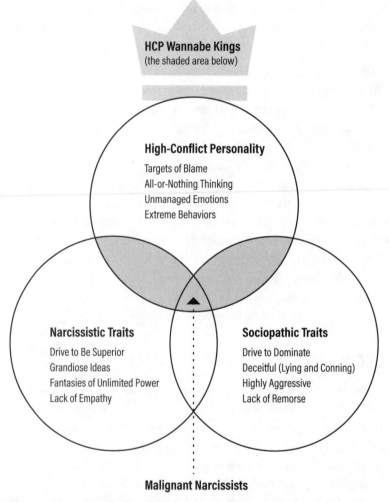

FIGURE 1. High-Conflict Politicians. *Copyright © 2019 Bill Eddy, All Rights Reserved,* Why We Elect Narcissists and Sociopaths—And How We Can Stop, *Berrrett-Koehler Publishers*

will find that these patterns get easier and easier to spot. Since HCPs don't change their behavior, they are, in fact, *more predictable* than the average person.

Remember, you are not diagnosing anyone; rather, you are watching out for those you do not want to assume positions of power over you—whether this is in relationships, at work, or as your political leaders.

HIGH-CONFLICT
EMOTIONAL WARFARE

One of the most surprising—and shocking and terrifying—things about all high-conflict people (HCPs) is that they attack those closest to them. From those who perpetrate domestic violence to the workplace bully to high-conflict politicians, HCPs turn against those who are on their same team: their family, their community, their party, their nation, and their allies. These are their *Targets of Blame*. They repeatedly criticize them, laugh at them, publicly ridicule them, damage their property, and harm their relationships; some HCPs even physically assault or kill their Targets of Blame.

I call this *high-conflict emotional warfare* because it's communicated emotionally, not rationally, and it triggers overwhelming emotions in their targets and those around them. It makes no sense logically to be attacked like this. Often HCP targets start to feel crazy and become immobilized. If you've ever been one, you know what it's like.

All HCPs engage in this. They are at war with the world—mostly the world around them. But HCP politicians do it on a much larger and more dangerous scale. These Wannabe Kings can't stop themselves in their endless effort to gain unlimited power. Here's how it works.

The High-Conflict Emotional Warfare Pattern

This pattern has four steps that I have identified:

1. **Seduce** Negative Advocates.

2. **Attack** Targets of Blame.

3. **Divide** their community.

4. **Dominate** everyone.

It's very important to learn this pattern so that when you are someone's Target of Blame, you can understand what is happening to you and that it is not something you caused. No one deserves this. Targets often don't know how to react because they never expected to be treated this way in a cooperative society. But HCPs have *highly aggressive behavior.* When you see them viciously attack someone else, be aware that sooner or later they may attack you too. They can't stop themselves, so others need to stop them.

Seducing Their Negative Advocates

The concept of *Negative Advocates* first arose for me in legal disputes, when I saw HCPs gathering family, friends, co-workers, neighbors, and others to advocate for their distorted thinking and to help them attack their Targets of Blame. Since they usually have no basis for most of their legal claims, these HCPs resorted to emotional pressure to win their cases. By bringing their Negative Advocates to court, they could make it appear that they had a strong case based on the credibility of these advocates and the size of their support.

However, since the legal process focuses on facts and evidence (in contrast to the political process), HCPs often lose because they don't really have a case. But with some juries and a few judges, they occasionally win their cases through emotional persuasion and the presence of their Negative Advocates.

In reversing the decision in a personal injury case, a court of appeals in Louisiana said the following, criticizing the emotional tactics of the lawyers (the Negative Advocates for an apparently HCP client):

> [T]rial counsel engaged in improper trial conduct and made improper closing arguments **to confuse and inflame the jury** . . . [this conduct] causes more than great concern. Counsel is cautioned that such conduct in the future will result in the imposition of severe sanctions. But, this

great concern goes beyond sanctions; the greatest concern is that counsel seems intent on winning at any cost, notwithstanding concomitant violations of long-established rules of practice and **in disregard, it seems, of the truth**.[31] (Emphasis added)

This case was decided in 1996, but the terms used by the court easily fits today's politics: "winning at any cost," "disregard of the truth," etc. Negative Advocates, when they are professionals such as lawyers, are often seen as more credible than the HCP. Yet these Negative Advocates can be ordinary people, too—people who become emotionally hooked but are uninformed. Once such people become informed, they often abandon HCPs and stop fighting for them. Since all of this is based on emotions, these advocates' support is fleeting. People regularly get hooked into advocating for HCPs and then later abandon them. This is why HCPs are always recruiting new Negative Advocates.

Narcissists and sociopaths are the most seductive personalities and are both skilled at gathering such advocates. They know how to tell the stories that get people to fall in love with them and support their fights against their targets. This is just as true in politics as it is in their romantic relationships. They want advocates to worship them and defend them, so they build an emotional relationship from the start. HCPs tell their potential Negative Advocates that they love them and they expect to be loved in return. It's not about politics or policies; it's really about emotional attention, intensity, and repetition.

Keep in mind that this is just an act Wannabe Kings put on. They do not really love their followers, nor do they care about their advocates' personal or political needs. For HCPs, it is all about gaining more power for themselves so that they can dominate a community or a nation. They will strike an unstated devil's bargain with their followers:

Give me all your power and I will pretend to love you and speak for you against the "establishment," the "elites," and the "invaders" of our great country. But everything I do is really just a tactic to gain power—over you and everyone else. I will discard you the moment you become inconvenient, disloyal, or expect anything in return.

In addition to seducing their Negative Advocates by telling them that they are special people, HCPs also promise an idyllic (and unrealistic) life. It appears that HCPs on the political right usually promise a return to the glorious past—usually a vanished agrarian paradise[32]—while HCPs on the left promise a glorious workers' future.[33]

For example, Hitler gave impassioned speeches that "especially the ladies" enjoyed. In 1922, an American reporter noted one woman who could not tear her eyes away:

> Transfixed as if in some devotional ecstasy, she had ceased to be herself and was completely under the spell of Hitler's despotic faith in Germany's future greatness.[34]

This future greatness was based on reclaiming an idyllic past—a time before Germany lost World War I and had to pay reparations to France. Hitler promised to make Germany great again. He was on the far right.

On the other hand, Stalin, on the far left, promised a great revolutionary time in the future, unlike any that had existed before, when factories and farms would be collectivized and would be run by the people instead of by the capitalists. In 1929, an American received a letter from a Russian friend who wrote with "ecstatic excitement." He was one of the young urban revolutionaries who went to the countryside to collectivize the farms:

> I am off in villages with a group of other brigadiers, organizing [collective farms]. It is a tremendous job, but we are making amazing progress . . . I am confident that in time not a peasant will remain on his own land. We shall yet smash the last vestiges of capitalism and forever rid ourselves of exploitation. . . . The very air here is afire with a new spirit and a new energy.[35]

Both these grandiose fantasies were created by HCP Wannabe Kings who had no trouble exaggerating and lying to people to gain power over them. These were the beginnings of stories that ended in war, famine, and genocide. Of those who survived the destruction that resulted, many infatuated followers later wrote memoirs of how they were misled.[36] In order for HCPs to accomplish their incredible goals, they seduce their followers into destroying their Targets of Blame.

Attacking Their Targets of Blame

While they are recruiting their Negative Advocates, HCPs are also constantly verbally attacking their Targets of Blame. This helps them establish a stronger bond with their Negative Advocates: *It's Us against Them!* They teach their advocates that their targets are evil, powerful, and plotting against them. HCP Wannabe Kings speak to their advocates in large groups at rallies to reinforce belonging to the group, following the leader, and hating their assigned targets. In addition, these rallies feed the narcissism of the Wannabe Kings and increase their drive rather than reduce it.

They also train their advocates to join in attacking their targets by leading chants and hinting at violence. It is in this way that they get their followers to do their dirty work while at the same time denying any responsibility for leading them and teaching them to do it. *It's just words,* they say.

Targets of Blame are usually caught off-guard and feel crazy. *What did I do to deserve this? I thought we were friends—a community of people with shared goals! Normal people don't treat their [family] [friends] [colleagues] [allies] this way!* A classic warfare example of this is when Hitler invaded Russia during World War II. Stalin was caught totally unprepared because he thought he and Hitler were friends and believed that Hitler would never do such a thing.[37] There's no honor among Wannabe Kings.

Dividing Their Community

When HCPs teach their advocates to attack their targets, this divisive behavior is part of a psychological process called *splitting.* This term has been associated with personality disorders for decades, including narcissists,[38] and it indicates that the person sees other people as either "all good" or "all bad," or simply as "winners" or "losers."[39] For HCPs, there's no in-between. When they communicate this splitting, they do it emotionally so that others absorb the split and start viewing the identified people as all good or all bad themselves—often without even realizing it.

Figure 2 shows what this HCP pattern looks like.

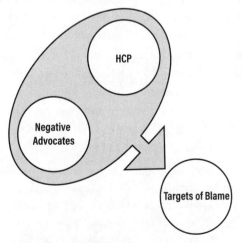

FIGURE 2. HCP Splitting. *Copyright © 2019 Bill Eddy, All Rights Reserved,* Why We Elect Narcissists and Sociopaths—And How We Can Stop, *Berrrett-Koehler Publishers*

By speaking constantly about these all-good or all-bad people, HCPs divide groups by spreading rumors, making veiled threats, pitting citizens against each other, and occasionally by switching sides to keep everyone else off balance. In a cooperative society, it's easy for HCPs to simply pick off individuals by attacking them publicly and blaming them for any problems they wish. This stirs up the whole community and causes everyone to make an emotional decision for or against that person. Since the targeted individual is not used to having to publicly defend themselves in a cooperative society, often they become terrified and immobilized.

Hitler provided the prototype for how to do this, which has been followed by almost all Wannabe Kings ever since. He called it the formula for "spiritual and physical terror," which he claimed he learned from another movement, but it describes his own approach exactly:

> I understood the infamous spiritual terror which this movement exerts, particularly on the bourgeoisie [middle class], which is neither morally nor mentally equal to such attacks; at a given sign it unleashes a veritable barrage of lies and slanders against whatever adversary seems most dangerous, until the nerves of the attacked persons break down . . . This is a tactic based on precise calculation of all human weaknesses, and its result will lead to success with almost mathematical certainty . . .[40]

In addition to such precise attacks, these Wannabe Kings easily shift sides, confusing and defusing their opponents. After one side in the group has submitted to them, they attack the other side. All the while, they blame these conflicts on others and deny all responsibility for what they have done. Stalin was apparently brilliant at doing this.

At first, after Lenin died in 1924, he organized support within the Communist Party against his main rival, Trotsky. He sided with the "Rightists," who tolerated a form of free commerce and peasants owning land, against the "Leftists," led by Trotsky, who saw this freedom for farmers as allowing capitalists to enrich themselves.

> But in 1927 he flipped his politics: having satisfactorily disposed of the "Leftists"—Trotsky was by now in disgrace, and would soon be in exile— Stalin now began preparing an attack on the "Rightists," Bukharin and the New Economic Policy. In other words, Stalin used the grain crisis, as well as the general economic dissatisfaction, not only to radicalize Soviet policy, but also to complete the destruction of this group of rivals.[41]

Dominating Everyone

This intense drive to have power over other people can be impulsive, automatic, and intuitive, and it doesn't turn off until the people or groups the Wannabe Kings are trying to dominate submit to them or are eliminated. Those who have become their Negative Advocates—their followers—are happy to submit to them. Those who the Wannabe Kings have targeted in their community either submit, leave, or are destroyed.

Conclusion

This way, one by one, Wannabe Kings gain power over everyone. Many people believe they will eventually stop themselves and become reasonable. But they are never satisfied and continue without self-restraint until they are stopped by a larger force (Hitler was only stopped by the Allies) or succumb to the limits of the human body (Stalin died from a stroke after more than thirty years in power).

But why don't people stop them early on, especially when some people see the HCP patterns when they can still be stopped?

THE 4-WAY VOTER SPLIT

When voters are exposed to the intensity of an HCP Wannabe King's emotional warfare, they tend to split into four groups (based on my observations and reading about historical and current leaders). This helps ensure the Wannabe King's election and domination. These groups are based on voter temperaments or personal emotional styles, not on any standard type of personality analysis or disorders. The groups are flexible so that depending on how they are treated, members may shift from one group to another, from one election to another.

The Four Groups

Here are the four groups who become divided or split by HCP Wannabe Kings:

LOVING LOYALISTS These are the HCP's followers who would do anything for their leader. Loyalists believe that their HCP is special and will serve their needs where others haven't. They believe their HCP speaks to them and for them. They generally agree with the HCPs attacks on their Targets of Blame.

The following three groups generally disagree with the HCP's attacks on their targets but have three different emotional reactions to it.

RILED-UP RESISTERS Resisters are the strong opponents, those who view the HCP's behavior as alarming and requiring strong opposition, otherwise the community or country will suffer dire consequences.

MILD MODERATES Moderates are the people who see the Wannabe King's behavior in generally political terms and vote for or against them based on parties or policies, mostly ignoring their character defects and attacks as minor or temporary.

DISENCHANTED DROPOUTS Dropouts are the people who most strongly dislike politics and want nothing to do with it. They don't think their vote matters, so they don't bother voting. They see the Wannabe King as being just like all the other politicians.

Figure 3 is what this 4-way split looks like.

The result of the HCP's emotional attacks is that *all* of the groups become highly emotional and fight with each other. This has the effect of further strengthening the Loyalists' ties to their HCP leader and neutralizing the three opposition groups. The following is a description of the emotional response pattern that is surprisingly consistent throughout the examples in this book:

LOVING LOYALISTS Loyalists despise Resisters for criticizing their leader and looking down on them. They hate the Resisters' resistance and consider them unpatriotic and possibly evil. They dismiss Moderates as simply representing the "establishment," since they tend to be those in the political center. Loyalists are emotionally inspired to follow.

RILED-UP RESISTERS Resisters despise the Loyalists and can't understand how they can support the Wannabe King. They think Loyalists are not very smart. Resisters are angry with Moderates for seeming unconcerned about the HCP and believe they are too willing to give in to their demands. Resisters are also angry with the Dropouts and say they should be ashamed of themselves for not voting. Resisters are emotionally inspired to fight.

MILD MODERATES Moderates dislike the extremes of the Loyalists who are challenging their moderate values. They also dislike the Resisters because they don't see the need for angry protests and are emotionally turned off by them. They are generally disappointed with the Dropouts.

Moderates tend to wring their hands about the polarization they see, but they don't know where it came from and how to reduce it. They are emotionally inspired to freeze.

DISENCHANTED DROPOUTS   Dropouts may dislike the aggressive nature of the Wannabe King, but they blame both the Loyalists and the Resisters for conflicts and polarization. Dropouts feel pressure from both camps to vote for their side, but they mostly ignore the "political" people and focus on their own lives. They are emotionally inspired to flee.

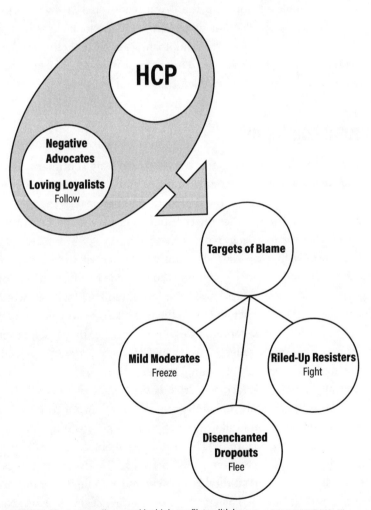

FIGURE 3. The 4-way split created by high-conflict politicians. *Copyright © 2019 Bill Eddy, All Rights Reserved, Why We Elect Narcissists and Sociopaths—And How We Can Stop, Berrrett-Koehler Publishers*

Wannabe Kings are skilled at keeping these groups fighting each other or immobilized by creating an ongoing sense of conflict, chaos, crisis, and fear. Through their constant speeches, they use what each group says and does to feed the anger of the other groups. This way they can gain power and remain in power.

Interestingly, they don't usually have the support of more than about 40 percent of the adult population (their Loyalists), so the other three groups combined (60 percent) could easily out-vote them if they united. Instead, these groups often stay divided and emotionally ineffective.

For an example of applying the 4-way voter split (shown earlier in Figure 3.1) to a specific election, go to Chapter 8 and look at the part titled "US Presidential Election—2016." And if you want to apply this framework to other examples in this book or to one of your own, refer to Appendix C; feel free to make a copy of the blank form for your own use.

Cultural Leadership

What most people don't see is that the Wannabe King is primarily responsible for keeping these fights and conflicts going, not the other groups. Polarization doesn't fall from the sky. As the cultural leader, the HCP has a powerful influence on whether the community or nation takes an adversarial or a cooperative approach to problem-solving.

It's almost like flipping a switch. A unifying leader will use words to overcome divisions and inspire a community to set aside its differences in order to accomplish a common task. A divisive leader (an HCP) will use words to pit people against each other and teach them to take action against individuals or groups within their communities. In this manner they teach polarization, rather than simply reflecting the views of the community. We will see this over and over again in the examples in Part II.

Ironically, an HCP leader can drive *both sides* of these conflicts. The HCP does this by attacking one of the split groups, then another, while flattering their followers. Although these opposition groups may not like the HCP, they still tend to absorb the HCP's opinion about the other opposition groups, which then affects their voting patterns. The four split groups are somewhat flexible so that cultural leaders can move some of them from one group to another. But the basic pattern of splitting seems to have existed throughout history.

Hitler's Example

Hitler built up his Nazi party of Negative Advocates (Loyalists) primarily by treating the small Jewish population in Germany (about 1 percent of the country at the time) as his Target of Blame. By the elections in February 1932, the Nazis had become the largest party in Germany having grown from a tiny regional group in the 1920s. They received approximately 42 percent of the seats in the Reichstag (parliament). The Social Democrats received 24 percent, the (Catholic) Center Party 18 percent, and the Communist Party 16 percent.[42]

The Social Democrats were in power at the time and were essentially the Mild Moderates, along with the Center Party. Hitler attacked the Social Democrats viciously as the establishment, blamed them for losing World War I, and falsely claimed they were controlled by Jews.

The German Communist Party (Riled-Up Resisters) was told by Stalin, in Communist Russia, to focus on attacking the Social Democrats, since he dismissed the Nazis as having little potential. The Social Democrats saw the Communists as the bigger threat, so these two groups weakened each other. The Center Party, with the cooperation of the Social Democrats, *eased* restrictions on the Nazis, which allowed them to get into bloody street fights with the Communists. It's unclear how many people (Dropouts) didn't vote in this February 1932 election.

In the November election later that year, the Nazis lost votes to become only 35 percent of the parliament, but because they were still the largest party, Hitler was appointed Chancellor in January 1933.[43] If the other parties could have recognized Hitler's Wannabe King patterns, instead of being focused on their long history of squabbling, they might have worked together and prevented World War II and the genocidal holocaust of the Jews and Hitler's other Targets of Blame.

Stalin's Example

In the 1930s, Stalin wanted to make the farms of the Soviet Union into large collectives so they would be more efficient at producing more grain to sell for industrial equipment.[44] At the same time, doing this would help the government stamp out any capitalist tendencies farmers might have developed by owning their own small farms ever since the Russian tsar gave the peasants their freedom in 1861.[45]

Stalin saw these resistant land-owning peasant farmers as his Targets of Blame. He called them *kulaks*—a rare term from before the revolution that "simply implied someone who was doing well, or someone who could afford to hire others to work, but not necessarily someone wealthy."[46]

> [One Soviet leader said:] "If the requisition meant civil war between the kulaks and the poorer elements of the villages, then long live this civil war!" . . . [T]he Bolsheviks were actively seeking to deepen divisions inside the villages, to use anger and resentment to further their policy.[47]

In one mandatory meeting with peasant farmers, a young revolutionary brigade "propagandist" from the city urged the peasants to sign up for the collective farm:

> "Come on! It's late," he urged us. "The sooner you sign in, the sooner you go home." No one moved. All sat silently. The chairman, bewildered and nervous, whispered something in the propagandist's ear . . . We kept our silence. This irritated the officials, especially the chairman. A moment after the propagandist finished his admonishment, the chairman rushed from behind the table, grabbed the first man before him, and shook him hard. "You . . . you, enemy of the people!" he shouted, his voice choking with rage. "What are you waiting for?"[48]

I picture these peasants—caught in the middle between angry Loyalists and angry Resisters—as the Moderates, who didn't really cooperate but didn't really fight back either. These divisions enabled Stalin to divide and conquer by using Loyalists (including the urban revolutionaries and some local villagers) to do much of the dirty work, including forcibly taking food and equipment from farm families without leaving them anything to eat. It was these actions that caused the famines, which led to the deaths of millions by 1933.[49] Yet, there were always more peasant Resisters and Moderates (and Dropouts who left for the big cities) than Loyalists.

Emotions Are Contagious

How could these HCP Wannabe Kings be so successful at gaining followers and intimidating their critics in a century with such rapid development of information, communication, and logical problem-solving? It's simple. They are more effective than anyone else at using *emotional communication* and *emotional relationships*. These techniques are totally automatic for Wannabe Kings.

After all, emotions are contagious. And "high" emotions—fear, panic, jealousy, resentment, anger, rage—are highly contagious. Mild emotions are, of course, part of everyday life and they help us make decisions, get along with others, and build meaningful relationships. But when emotions run high, they get our hearts racing, our minds focused narrowly, and our muscles ready to fight, flee, or freeze. They also shut off the logical, problem-solving part of our brains so fast that we don't even realize it.

Brain researchers tell us that we can "catch" each other's emotions, *especially* when we are anxious. There are two parts of the brain in particular that play a big part in this. One is the *amygdala*:

> [T]he amygdala spots signs of fear in someone else's face with remarkable speed, picking it up in a glimpse as quick as 33 milliseconds, and in some people even in a mere 17 milliseconds…so fast that **the conscious mind remains oblivious** to that perception (though we might sense the resulting vague stirring of uneasiness). We may not consciously realize how we are synchronizing [with the other person], yet we mesh with remarkable ease.[50]

The other part is *mirror neurons*, which causes us to exhibit or rehearse in our brains and bodies the same behavior that we have seen in someone else, without even consciously thinking about it. They say that this is the primary way that children learn, as well as the reason adults can quickly join together in group action.

> [T]hese systems "allow us to grasp the minds of others not through conceptual reasoning but through direct simulation; **by feeling, not by thinking.**"
>
> This triggering of parallel circuitry in two brains lets us instantly achieve a shared sense of what counts in a given moment.[51] (Emphasis added)

In addition, brain research tells us that in the absence of a clear understanding of who is in power in a given situation, the person with the most emotionally expressive face usually commands the attention of the group.[52] Overall, it appears that our brains follow emotionally expressive leaders, just as we fall in love with emotionally expressive romantic partners. And in both situations, our emotional attractions operate outside of our conscious radar. We simply fall in love.

Narcissists and sociopaths intuitively know this and seduce people all the time. Groups follow them because they are emotionally expressive. But they don't actually care about their followers. It is only later that individuals and groups discover that they have been manipulated and misled. At that point, they are often too ashamed to admit it and may deny they have been misled.

For example, one of Stalin's young revolutionaries later expressed deep regrets when he realized how he had been misled by Stalin and his cohorts to contribute to the starvation of thousands of peasants when they tried to force collective farming on them. He described himself as succumbing "to a form of intellectual blindness" at the time.

> "To spare yourself mental agony you veil unpleasant truths from view by half-closing your eyes—and your mind. You make panicky excuses and shrug off knowledge with words like exaggeration and hysteria. . . . We spoke of the 'peasant front' and 'kulak menace,' 'village socialism' and 'class resistance.' In order to live with ourselves we had to smear the reality out of recognition with verbal camouflage."[53]

This emotional contagion can and does happen to everyone. We are actually all seduced into becoming emotional, although in different ways: some of us *fight*, some *flee*, some *freeze*, and some *follow*. The lesson to be learned here is that we need to watch out for this occurring and work together, rather than simply accept the emotional messages of those leaders who seem to be on "our side" when they say that it is a case of "us against them."

Emotional Differences

It's also important to understand that people in different political groups may have a predisposition to think more one way than another. Part of what allows us as voters to be split and to argue with each other is the assumption that when people disagree with us they are stupid or evil. However, it turns out that our individual brains may be predisposed to see things differently—perhaps from birth.[54]

For example, some people seem to be born with the tendency to value loyalty highly, follow authority, have empathy for one's own group, be suspicious of strangers, and seek certainty and stability. These people are generally more conservative. Others seem to be born to seek novelty and change, to be interested in people who look different, and to have empathy for strangers in need. They are generally more liberal. [55]

These conservative-liberal personality differences seem to exist even outside of politics. For example, Republicans apparently have three times as many nightmares as Democrats.[56] And liberals "are more likely to own travel books than conservatives."[57] Studies have shown that as early as four years old, children have already begun to show these differing personality tendencies.[58]

Three political science researchers have been studying the biology and psychology of political orientations. They believe that a lot of our behavioral tendencies may be inborn, including some liberal and conservative personality traits. They found that what you gaze at, what disgusts you, and who attracts you as a mate are among the many traits that correspond somewhat with political tendencies. "Slices of the population on both the political left and the political right are predisposed, and therefore for all intents and purposes unpersuadable."[59]

Others agree that whether our political personalities developed primarily from genetics, early childhood upbringing, or cultural experience, they appear mostly set by adulthood.

> [Most] people either inherit their party affiliations from their parents, or they form an attachment to one party or another early in adulthood. Few people switch parties once they hit middle age. . . . Once they have formed an affiliation, people bend their philosophy and their perceptions of reality so they become more and more aligned with members of their political tribe.[60]

However, much of the time, people with these differing political tendencies get along just fine. It's when a Wannabe King enters the picture and repeatedly exaggerates these differences, purposefully dividing people, that it can become a serious problem. What's one of the most powerful tools they have for dividing people?

Fear Factor

Fear appears to be the strongest emotion that drives this split among voters. "Brain imaging studies have even shown that the fear center of the brain, the amygdala, is actually larger in conservatives than in liberals."[61] It is commonly said that a conservative is a liberal who has been mugged. And it is true that a liberal will temporarily become more conservative when "tired, hungry, rushed, distracted, or disgusted."[62]

On the other hand, a study at Yale University focused on the views of liberals and conservatives when they imagined a fearful situation such as flying in airplanes and then imagined being completely safe. After the flying experiment, liberals and conservatives reported the typical differences on social issues, apparently because flying increased a sense of fear. "But if they had instead just imagined being completely physically safe, the Republicans became significantly more liberal—their positions on social attitudes were much more like the Democratic respondents."[63]

While many politicians may say that power comes from organizing ability or good policies, Wannabe Kings emphasize fear or terror, as Hitler explained in his step-by-step method in Chapter 2. One Russian-born author, Masha Gessen, recently said this while analyzing Vladimir Putin's presidency and history: "Ideology was essential only at the very beginning, for the future totalitarian rulers to seize power. After that, terror kicked in."[64]

In the United States in 2018, it's interesting that a book came out titled *Fear: Trump in the White House,* in which the author, Bob Woodward quoted candidate Donald Trump as saying: "Real power is—I don't even want to use the word—fear."[65]

Remember it's not about the politics; it's about the personality.

Conclusion

In reality, it seems that a family, workplace, community, and country need both liberals and conservatives to balance each other's novelty seeking and stability seeking, openness to strangers and caution about strangers, loyalty to leaders and skepticism of leaders, and sensitivity to fear. But HCP Wannabe Kings use *emotional warfare*—they seduce, attack, divide, and dominate—to create chaos, conflict, confusion, and fear as a manipulative way to gain power for themselves.

When the Wannabe Kings are on the far left, the Loyalists tend to be liberal and the Resisters tend to be conservative (although there are some aghast liberals). Likewise, when the Wannabe Kings are on the far right, the Loyalists tend to be conservative and the Resisters tend to be liberal (and some aghast conservatives). Remember, these are primarily emotional tendencies.

Since we have different hard-wired or learned responses to this emotional warfare, we instinctively react with fight, flight, freeze, or follow. We fall into the trap of disagreeing with each other when we could unite and stop Wannabe Kings from ever getting elected. But why is this seemingly obvious manipulation increasing in the twenty-first century rather than fading away?

HIGH-EMOTION MEDIA

O ver the past three decades, the technology of media has undergone a huge change. At least seven seismic shifts have laid the groundwork for the recent increase in HCPs who want to be the center of attention and in charge of everything and everyone in their communities or countries:

1. FACE AND VOICE NEWS   For centuries, print media—newspapers, magazines, and books—were our primary sources of news and useful information. Not anymore. Now we have largely shifted away from the written word and back to the highly emotional realm of faces and voices.

Television, radio, movies, streaming video, and social media all communicate strong face and voice emotions much more than they communicate the details required for thoughtful problem-solving. Today, even newspapers and magazines provide us with plenty of faces and voices on their websites and in their podcasts.

It's not that old-fashioned books, magazines, and newspapers can't be highly emotional. (Think of Thomas Paine's *Common Sense*, or Adolf Hitler's *Mein Kampf*.) It's just that they are such frequent sources of useful information and guidance that most readers can immediately spot and recognize a passage or headline that is highly dramatic.

As described in Chapter 3, emotions are contagious and they can slip into our brains without our conscious awareness. Figure 4 shows how I imagine the information now flowing into our minds (Simply put: left brain generally processes words, right brain generally processes facial expressions and tone of voice. This is unrelated to political left and right.):

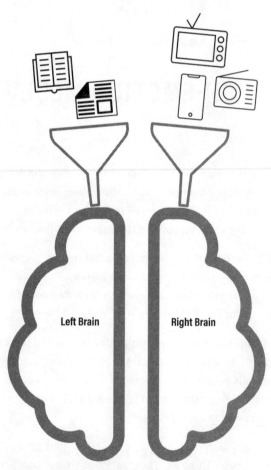

FIGURE 4. Rational media vs. emotional media. *Copyright © 2019 Bill Eddy, All Rights Reserved, Why We Elect Narcissists and Sociopaths—And How We Can Stop, Berrrett-Koehler Publishers*

2. MEDIA COMPETITION Modern media outlets have exploded during the past thirty years with cable TV, the internet, community TV, and social media all competing with the major networks and TV stations. And there's no more Walter Cronkite thoughtfully deciding what news we need to see. Instead, all of these media outlets—from the most thoughtful and careful to the outright sociopathic—compete for "market share."

To come out ahead in this competition, many media outlets often show the most extreme, attention-getting, bad behavior they can. The goal is to grab people by their emotions (especially using intense faces and voices).

3. HIGH-EMOTION MEDIA CRAVES HIGH-CONFLICT PERSONALITIES More than ever before, our media outlets now largely focus on personalities and what they say about each other and do to each other. Which personalities? Those who can best grab our attention. Those who show extreme charm and confidence. And those who consistently hold our interest with mood swings, unpredictable behavior, and a preoccupation with blaming others. Sound familiar?

Our modern high-emotion media outlets highlight—and crave—high-conflict personalities. And, remember, on the preconscious level, so do we. To ensure our survival, our brains are wired to focus on conflict, crisis, chaos, and fear over everything else. As a result, we naturally pay more attention to simple stories of heroes and villains, potential threats and attacks, victories and defeats. These are the very stories that HCPs consistently feed us—casting themselves as the heroes.

4. DRAMA DAY AND NIGHT With our modern digital technology, we can watch movies and TV shows on demand at any time of day or night—even during work hours—and for as many hours as we want. We can also play video games for hours. Adults now spend an average of eleven hours in front of screens every day.[66] Yes, part of that may be for work.

But much of what we consume via our screens is fantasy drama—made-up stories of heroes and villains, Grand Theft Auto video games, world war games, evil monsters, and marvelous superheroes. And the theme of much of this drama is *adversarial* conflict resolution. There's a terrible crisis! There's an evil villain! And there's an incredible superhero who will beat the crap out of our opponents! Basically, more feeling, less thinking.

5. IT'S VERY PERSONAL   Today's media outlets allow individual politicians to communicate with us directly in a very intimate, personal way. They can speak to us in our living room or bedroom, their faces filling the screen and their voices surrounding us with compelling words. And as we've seen, narcissists and sociopaths are supremely skilled at intimate seduction—figuring out what we want to hear, and then telling us exactly what we want to hear—and then manipulation. They can sense our vulnerabilities and strike fear in our hearts or tell us how special we are. Usually they do both.

In the 1930s, Adolf Hitler spoke to many millions of Germans in their own homes by radio on a regular basis. In the 1950s, Joseph McCarthy reached into most American homes that had TV with broadcasts of his hearings on Communists in our government (although he never found a single one). In the 2016 United States presidential election and throughout the first two years of his presidency, Donald Trump tweeted almost every day. Those tweets not only got retweeted but repeated by most major news media, partly because they were from the world's most powerful human being, partly because they were so bizarre and emotionally exciting, and partly because they helped each media outlet grow market share. It appears that with each new invention of a method of intimate mass communication, the public initially gives it extra power and significance—until we discover how easily it can be used to manipulate us and start to set limits on its power.

6. YET IT'S ALSO VERY VIRAL   The speed at which today's face and voice media can send emotional messages is astonishing. Facebook, YouTube, Twitter, and other social media platforms have developed an incredible capacity to spread political messages—true and false—ricocheting around the globe. A major study showed that false emotional news spreads farther and faster.

False news reached more people than the truth; the top 1% of false news cascades diffused to between 1000 and 100,000 people, whereas the truth rarely diffused to more than 1000 people. Falsehood also diffused faster than the truth. The degree of novelty and the emotional reactions of recipients may be responsible for the differences observed.[67]

One of the biggest issues in the 2016 US presidential election was whether foreign governments—notably Russia—had assisted in manipulating voters into believing false news. National correspondents have commented that "Without Facebook, Donald Trump probably wouldn't be president. . . . The platform was an essential vector for Russian disinformation.[68]

In the Philippines, fake news spread on social media is credited with contributing to the election of Rodrigo Duterte.

[T]he internet in the Philippines of Mr. Duterte has become an outlet for threats and deceit. . . . Facebook [is] the source of almost all internet news in the Philippines. It's a losing battle—false news is so rooted in the Philippines that one Facebook executive has called it "patient zero" in the global misinformation epidemic.[69]

7. IMPAIRED ABILITY TO THINK   It's not just the information promoted by today's media, but it's the process of watching as well. As Marshall McLuhan used to say, "the medium is the message."[70] Here's how our screens impact us:

Screens are insatiable. At a cognitive level, they are voracious vampires for your attention, and as soon as you look at one, you are basically toast. There are studies that bear this out. One, by a team led by Adrian Ward, a marketing professor at the University of Texas' business school, found that the mere presence of a smartphone within glancing distance can **significantly reduce your cognitive capacity**.[71] (Emphasis added)

All of these trends have made today's high-conflict politicians far more emotionally powerful than any HCP Wannabe King in the past. Emotional warfare is now the name of the game in modern politics. And it all operates beneath our logical radar, intimately passed on to thousands and millions of people at a time, 24 hours a day, 7 days a week.

Welcome to the Future and the Past

Because of the rise of high-emotion media, many of us have started to view the world in highly emotional terms: primarily as a dangerous, adversarial place in which we desperately need heroes to protect us from many villains. Just like in the old days.

Yet this is mostly untrue. Overall, today our lives are less dangerous than ever before (with some notable exceptions). In general, most of us experience less war, less poverty, and generally live longer and healthier lives than in any earlier era.[72] It just *feels* more dangerous and frightening. Why? Because of our high-emotion media over the past thirty years and because of the Wannabe Kings who use it to frighten and manipulate us.

> Consumers of negative news, not surprisingly, become glum: a recent literature review cited "misperception of risk, anxiety, lower mood levels, learned helplessness, contempt and hostility towards others, desensitization, and in some cases, . . . complete avoidance of the news." And they become fatalistic, saying things like "Why should I vote? It's not gonna help . . . "[73]

And when we *feel* this frightened, this fear creates an ideal opening for HCPs to step forward, build followings, and grab power. Remember, as I said in Chapter 3, when people feel anxious, they are more likely to absorb other people's emotions—especially high-conflict emotions.

In addition, the constant negativity in the media changes people's political mood to embrace more extreme solutions:

> For decades, journalism's steady focus on problems and seemingly incurable pathologies was preparing the soil that allowed Trump's seeds of discontent and despair to take root. . . . One consequence is that many Americans today have difficulty imagining, valuing or even believing in the promise of incremental change, which leads to a greater appetite for revolutionary, smash-the-machine change.[74]

Our Political Culture of Blame

Our current political culture of blame also began in the 1990s. For the fifty years before that, Americans (and people throughout much of the free world) had a shared enemy—a frightening, powerful, and bitter enemy. That enemy was the Soviet Union (or the USSR). For most of those five decades, the US and the USSR had thousands of nuclear missiles aimed directly at each other.

Then, in 1989, the Berlin Wall came down and the Soviet Union collapsed over the next couple years. It literally ceased to exist. In its place were many independent, but generally weak, nations. Suddenly, the nuclear threat from all of the former Soviet countries decreased dramatically. Just as suddenly, among Americans, the decades of justifiable fear, anger, and blame had no target.

Then a strange thing started to happen. Americans began turning inward to find new enemies to blame and fear—and they discovered them at home and next door.

As a result, national politics began changing as well. Year by year, especially on the national level, our elected officials became less and less collegial, and more and more rancorous and obstructive. Instead of having lunch together in the Senate Dining Room, Democrats and Republicans declared the opposing party their sworn enemy. They stopped spending as much time together, both personally and politically. Adversarial thinking replaced the compromise and collaboration of the past, even including the Ronald Reagan and Tip O'Neill era of cooperation in the 1980s.

Some credit Newt Gingrich, a congressman from South Carolina who eventually became Speaker of the House, for changing the tone.

> By 1988, Gingrich's plan to conquer Congress via sabotage was well under way. . . . Gingrich encouraged them to go after their enemies with catchy, alliterative nicknames—"Daffy Dukakis," "the loony left"—and schooled them in the art of partisan blood sport. Through GOPAC, he sent out cassette tapes and memos to Republican candidates across the country who wanted to "speak like Newt," providing them with carefully honed attack lines and creating, quite literally, a new vocabulary for a generation of conservatives. One memo, titled "Language: A Key Mechanism of Control," included a list of recommended words to use in describing Democrats: *sick, pathetic, lie, anti-flag, traitors, radical, corrupt.*[75]

Now, on the national level at least, though often at other levels as well, it's largely about fundraising for the next election. It's also, of course, about winning—defeating the enemy in the opposing party. So, as a politician, you'd better be a fighter. Politics has again become a job for which HCPs are especially well qualified.

The Media and Politics

In 1979, C-SPAN began providing live television coverage of congressional proceedings, as well as many other forms of political programming. Two years later, Judge Joseph Wapner and Court TV transformed our view of the legal system as well. What had been private decision-making quickly became emotional public entertainment. Newt Gingrich was one of the first to make good use of it.

> He recognized an opportunity in the newly installed C-SPAN cameras, and began delivering tirades against Democrats to an empty chamber, knowing that his remarks would be beamed to viewers across the country. . . .

The goal was to reframe the boring policy debates in Washington as a national battle between good and evil, white hats versus black—a fight for the very soul of America. Through this prism, any news story could be turned into a wedge.[76]

Another big change came a few years later: the end of the *fairness doctrine*. This had been instituted by the Federal Communications Commission (FCC) in 1949 to require radio and television stations to provide a balance of political opinions. This meant that their programs on politics were required to include opposing opinions on whatever topic was under discussion.

The rule also required broadcasters to alert anyone who was subject to a personal attack in their programming and to give them an opportunity to respond. In addition, it required any broadcasters who endorsed political candidates to invite other candidates to speak.

The FCC began to reconsider this rule in the mid-80s and stopped enforcing it in 1987. (The rule was officially scrapped in 2011.) This meant that by the 1990s, any radio or TV station (or network) could state its own point of view as strongly and as repeatedly as it wished—and that it had no obligation to ever provide its audience with any other viewpoint.[77]

This change resulted in the explosion of political talk radio in the late 80s and early 90s. Then, in 1996, this naturally led to the creation and rise of the cable news channels Fox News and MSNBC—and, of course, to many other equally partisan media outlets.

During the past three decades, many of these outlets have spread an us-against-them view of the world. Welcome back to the simplified world of heroes and villains.

No one better understood how to encourage this us-against-them mentality, or how to use it to grab and hold people's attention, than Roger Ailes, the founder of Fox News. As Gabriel Sherman noted in his book *The Loudest Voice in the Room*,

Ailes remade both American politics and media. More than anyone of his generation, he helped transform politics into mass entertainment—monetizing the politics while making entertainment a potent organizing force. . . . Through Fox, Ailes helped polarize the American electorate, drawing sharp, with-us-or-against-us lines, demonizing foes, preaching against compromise.[78]

Ailes also made news sexy. He understood and proved that television—including politically oriented television—is built on good drama and plenty of blame. And well-funded political divisions, when turned into personal attacks and the public exposure of private lives, can provide plenty of both, especially when a sex scandal is involved. The Fox Network made a name for itself with its coverage of the Bill Clinton sex scandal and impeachment of the 1990s.[79]

By 2002, Fox was the number one cable news network. Its audience soon grew to more than twice that of CNN and MSNBC. It has held this lead for most of the last two decades.[80]

Cultural Leaders

Soon, other TV networks—and other media outlets in general—decided that they needed to adopt some of Fox News's aggressive style. During the Obama administration, *The New York Times*'s managing editor, Jill Abramson, said, "The narrative was being hijacked by Fox. Fox had taken over a thought-leader role in the national press corps." She acknowledged that the *Times*'s reporting style would need to become slightly more like Fox's in the future.[81]

Roger Ailes became a cultural leader without even being in political office.

> "Political conflict has never been more compelling than on Ailes's Fox News. . . . Though marketed as an antidote to the epistemic closure of the mainstream media, Fox News is as closed off as the media world it proposes to balance—**Ailes's audience seldom watches anything else**.[82] (Emphasis added)

This is a good time to introduce the concept of *emotional repetition in isolation*. Most people realize that when we are exposed to emotional information repeatedly, it is easily absorbed without thinking. TV advertising is based on this principle. But when it comes to politics and cultural issues, people have traditionally been exposed to many sources of information, in their neighborhoods, their workplaces, and city or regional newspapers.

As newspapers are vanishing and cable TV is all pervasive (as well as Facebook and other social media), the risks of getting political information from only one source is significant—and dangerous, as the examples in Part II demonstrate.

> On Fox News, the tedious personages of workaday politics are reborn as **heroes and villains** with triumphs and reverses—never-ending story lines. And the beauty of it is that Ailes's viewers—the voters—are the protagonists, victims of socialist overlords, or rebels coming to take the government

back. The viewers, on their couches, are flattered as the most important participants, the foot soldiers in Ailes's army.[83] (Emphasis added)

Other media, including the *Times*, have slowly focused more and more on negative news, reinforcing the *feeling* that things are bad and getting worse. Yet overall things in the world are better than ever according to objective research:

> *The New York Times* got steadily more morose from the early 1960s to the early 1970s, lightened up a bit (but just a bit) in the 1980s and 1990s, and then sank into a progressively worse mood in the first decade of the new century. News outlets in the rest of the world, too, became gloomier and gloomier from the late 1970s to the present day. . . .[84]

> And here is a shocker: *The world has made spectacular progress in every single measure of human well-being.* Here is the second shocker: *Almost no one knows about it.*

> Information about human progress, though absent from major news outlets and intellectual forums, is easy enough to find.[85]

As a result, many—perhaps most—Americans now routinely view politics as crisis-driven and a zero-sum game in which only one side wins and the other side has to lose. As described earlier, many people have just one news source, resulting in political messages with endless emotional repetition in isolation.

Always Adversarial Leadership

Over the past thousand years, kings (and queens) have been slowly replaced by written rules and laws—from the Magna Carta of 1215 that limited a king's power[86] to the United States Constitution of 1789 to the spread of constitutional governments around the world. Thoughtful consideration of written information has prevailed. In current times, collaboration and teamwork have become the primary methods of decision-making and managing everyday life in our complex and interconnected world.

With this recent return to emotional face and voice media that shares increasingly negative news to grab people's attention and market share, we are going backward a thousand years or more in our leadership approach—especially national leadership worldwide—to the times of always adversarial Wannabe Kings. Table 1 describes this shift.

TABLE 1: Political Leadership

	ALWAYS ADVERSARIAL (HEROES AND VILLAINS)	MODERN COLLABORATION (TEAMWORK)
Foundation for society	The king, with his whims and edicts	The constitution, with its laws and rules
Leaders chosen by	Brute force, emotional warfare, inherited power	Regular elections, policies and persuasion, leadership experience
Leaders need to be	Good at fighting Top-down, dictatorial	Good at collaborating Motivational, democratic
Communication by	Face and voice (Lots of emotion)	Mostly writing (Lots of information)
Decision-making by	Gut feelings	Research and analysis
Problems are caused by	Bad people (villains)	Multiple causes (sometimes bad behaviors)
Solutions are	Lock up or eliminate bad people. Heroes will do it all for you. All-or-nothing solutions	Get people to change their behavior. Punish bad behavior when necessary. Inspiring leadership, activating creativity and effort of others Complex, interrelated solutions

Conclusion

The result of our high-emotion media is that voters have been primed to think in terms of always adversarial drama—with crises, villains, and heroes—that fits ancient times more than the present. In today's world, this is a *Fantasy Crisis Triad*. In the past, people would have laughed at leaders promoting such fantasies, but over the past thirty years, the high-emotion media has made this all possible again, as the next chapter explains.

THE FANTASY CRISIS TRIAD

How do high-conflict narcissists and sociopaths—our HCP Wannabe Kings—persuade so many people to vote for them given how dangerous and deceptive they can be?

We have learned that they communicate primarily emotionally and that the high-emotion media powerfully enhances their messages. But *what* do they communicate that makes people give them so much power?

First, they start by convincing you that there is a terrible crisis. They may believe it themselves or they may know that they're making it up. Either way, the HCP's strategy is the same.

In a crisis, we think differently than we do when we are doing ordinary problem-solving, because there's no time to think. We just need to *act*. We fight, flee, freeze, or follow!

Also, in a crisis, we usually have to work together. In order to work together most efficiently, we need to have a leader—someone who can show us the way and tell us what to do.

In a crisis, we are willing to give up our individuality—to shut down our independent thinking—in order to save our skins. This is why every army has a chain of command that must be strictly followed. So, in a crisis, we follow the leader automatically. It's part of our social DNA.

Stop Thinking

Here's an example of how history's most infamous HCP—Adolf Hitler—got the German people to stop thinking and believe in a crisis that was actually a fantasy.

Edgar Mowrer, an American reporter in Germany in the 1930s, reported the following conversation:

> "Everybody in Germany knows that the Jews are our misfortune," one of the Nazis replied.
>
> "But just how? Why?" Edgar persisted.
>
> "There are too many of them. And then, Jews are not people like the rest of us."
>
> "But in my country the proportion of Jews is much higher than in Germany. But we lost no war, have not starved, not been betrayed to foreigners; in short, have suffered none of the evils you attribute to the presence of the Jews in Germany. How do you account for this?"
>
> "We don't account for it. We simply know it is true," the Nazi replied.
>
> "Is that logical, is that clear thinking?"
>
> "*Ach*, thinking!" the exasperated Nazi replied. "We are sick of thinking. Thinking gets you nowhere. The *Fuhrer* himself says true Nazis think with their blood."
>
> And this lack of thinking was everywhere.[87]

Hitler created a fantasy crisis with a fantasy villain—Jews—and a fantasy hero—himself.

Likewise, at Donald Trump's presidential inauguration, Trump insisted that America was facing "carnage" (which he didn't define). Then he uttered a classic Wannabe King line: "I alone can fix it." (On hearing this, former President George W. Bush allegedly said aloud, "That was some weird s--t!"[88])

Today's real problems can rarely, if ever, be fixed by one person. That's why modern politicians and presidents need to have many skills including cooperation, complex problem-solving, leading, and inspiring the efforts of others. They can't just dominate others to solve problems in the real modern world.

Everything's a Crisis

HCPs tend to see most crises—whether they are real or invented—in very simple terms: someone or some group is the sole cause (the villain), and that person or group needs to be controlled, removed, or destroyed. That person or group then becomes the Wannabe King's *Target of Blame*. All of this is part of the HCP's all-or-nothing thinking and extreme behavior. For them, problems don't have nuances and complex parts. The enemy just needs to be destroyed or defeated.

In ancient times, when the dangers included a pack of wolves or a boatful of Viking invaders, this approach often worked. It was always an adversarial world, even for us humans: kill or be killed, eat or be eaten. In addition to having Targets of Blame just like modern-day HCPs, the ancient narcissistic HCPs persuaded everyone that they were the greatest of leaders and that everyone should follow them. The sociopathic HCPs conned people into following them and ruthlessly fighting their real or supposed enemies. As a result, they became the leaders of their villages and eventually kings of the kingdoms.

To persuade people to follow them, Wannabe Kings employ what I call the *crisis triad*:

- There's a terrifying crisis!

- The cause is a hideous villain, who is totally evil and must be destroyed.

- We need to follow a wonderful hero, who will vanquish the villain and solve the crisis quickly.

This crisis can be entirely real, totally manufactured by the Wannabe King, or something in between.

High-conflict politicians seem to innately know this drama—and how to use it—in their blood and bones. They have an instinctive talent for declaring (or manufacturing) a crisis, defining a villain (or a group of villains), and promoting themselves as the heroes everyone desperately needs.

Although the crisis triad may have helped ancient adversarial leaders deal with some genuine crises, today very few real crises require us to stop thinking and simply and blindly follow one leader as we fight, flee, or freeze. Today's problems often require research, analysis, and many trained experts calmly (as much as possible) working together.

Table 2 shows the difference between real crises, real problems to solve, and pure fantasies. (See Part 2 for the stories behind many of these fantasy "crises.")

TABLE 2: Types of "Crises"

	REAL CRISES	FANTASY "CRISIS" (BUT REAL PROBLEM TO SOLVE)	PURE FANTASY "CRISIS" (NOT EVEN A PROBLEM TO SOLVE)
Nature of problem?	Tidal waves, fires, sexual assault, active shooter, etc.	Immigration policies, trade agreements, tax policies, environmental regulations, drug addiction, etc.	Jews in Germany; kulaks in Russia and Ukraine; Communists in the US federal government; "propaganda of homosexuals" in modern Russia; trade imbalance with Canada and US
How should we respond?	We don't have time to think; we just fight, flee, or freeze in place.	We should spend the time to think, analyze, collaborate with experts, and get many points of view on solving these problems.	We should not waste any time, energy, or resources on these total fantasies.
Should we stop thinking and blindly follow a leader?	Yes! Follow the leader and the instructions they give.	Combined knowledge and viewpoints are necessary; no one person is smart enough to solve these modern problems.	Don't follow (or vote for) any leaders or instructions based on these total fantasies.

Fantasy Villains

Unfortunately, over the past thirty years, many of our movies, news sources, and political parties, in addition to our culture of blame in general, have taught us that our problems—including some of our real problems—are simply caused by evil villains. These villains might be specific individuals, foreigners, people who think or look or talk or live differently than us, members of the opposing political party, and so forth. With intense and frequent emotional repetition, the media essentially *advertises* (for free) the Wannabe King's interpretation of events—their Fantasy Crisis Triad.

Fantasy Heroes

We're also mistakenly taught that problems and crises are mostly solved by *individual* heroes. We're mildly interested in groups of people who work together heroically, such as a platoon of soldiers in battle or the first responders to a natural disaster. But we're especially awed by unique *individual* heroes—certain special human beings who are exceptionally powerful, insightful, strong, or talented.

Don't believe any of this promotion. You're being set up to follow HCPs and their simplistic all-or-nothing thinking. That's where politicians, celebrities, and newscasters often eagerly join in. They tell us who the villains and heroes are—or, at least, who they should be. Usually they also tell us that the problem and the solution are simple, because they don't have much air time to explain anything in detail. They then repeat and repeat and repeat these simple problems, their equally simple solutions, and the names of the clear-cut villains based on what they have been told by the HCP politicians they interview.

These Wannabe Kings also continuously repeat that *they* are the heroes everyone wants and needs—and the sole human beings with the ability to vanquish the villains. Because of the reach and speed of modern media, this simple drama then ripples quickly around the nation and the world. Even media outlets that recognize its bogus nature help spread it, because it's considered news to be repeated—simply because it comes from a dramatic and compulsively verbal Wannabe King.

Over time, each Fantasy Crisis Triad feels more and more real. Eventually it takes hold, infecting us like a virus.

Two Responses to Human Problems

Our politicians regularly tell us how strong they are and how hard they will fight for us, which is fine: strength, commitment, and perseverance *are* all important. Often, they are precisely what we need.

Just as often, though, what we need instead—or in addition—are wisdom, creativity, nimbleness, vision, an ability to analyze complex problems, and a talent for building and maintaining alliances.

Although some problems can and should be solved by fighting and overcoming an enemy, most of today's problems can't begin to be addressed until people *stop* fighting. For our survival, we need to be able to think and act in both ways. Indeed, our brains are wired to operate in both. But not both at the same time.

Table 3 is a comparison of these two ways of addressing problems.

Table 3: Solving Real Human Problems

FLEXIBLE PROBLEM SOLVING	CRISIS REACTING
You approach the situation as a problem to solve or address.	Your response can only be all or nothing—you fight, flee, or freeze.
Your feelings are mild so you can concentrate.	The situation *feels* dire and extreme, whether it actually is or not.
You understand the importance of analyzing the problem.	You intuitively understand that survival lies in fast action, not analysis.
You see the problem as potentially complex, involving multiple aspects.	You see the problem as bad or evil people who must be avoided or destroyed.
You recognize the larger context in which the problem appears and understand that any response may have ripple effects and larger consequences.	You deal with the problem in isolation from other problems, issues, and contexts.
You see compromise as normal, so you are flexible and open to a wide range of solutions and approaches.	You see compromise as weak, dangerous, and possibly life-threatening.
You are able to manage your fear and anger and recognize that these emotions can interfere with making wise decisions.	Fear and anger are all-consuming and can only be relieved by reacting quickly, decisively, and perhaps overwhelmingly.

The way our brains are hardwired, only one of these approaches is dominant at any given time. We literally can't access both approaches at once; that is how and why high-conflict politicians often trick us and bend us to their will.

Nuances of the Fantasy Crisis Triad

Most high-conflict politicians either invent a crisis or take a real problem that needs to be solved and blow it out of proportion into something far more threatening; people then confuse this conflated problem with a crisis that requires them to blindly follow the leader.

And that's why it's so important to scrutinize their ostensible villain and hero.

If the villain is clearly and simply defined—that is, Mexicans, Jews, Republicans, Democrats, gays and lesbians, China, Communists, corporations, fat cats, Muslims, fascists, political correctness, capitalists, or straight white men—consider this to be a huge red flag. The candidate doing the finger pointing is very likely an HCP. Remember their character trait of all-or-nothing thinking.

Another reliable sign of a Fantasy Crisis Triad is if the candidate discourages any real analysis, debate, or examination of the facts. That's what Hitler did in the earlier example to get so many Germans to blindly follow him. He was able to distract the German people from thinking—about the absurdity that Jews were the evil and powerful villains he said they were—so they just believed him.

The biggest and clearest giveaway, though, is the third part of the triad: *I and only I can solve the problem.* The Wannabe King rarely talks about analyzing the problem and addressing it through cooperation, strategic alliances, or any other joint effort. Instead, they insist that no one else running for the office—perhaps no one else on the planet—has the wondrous ability to make everything better. They and only they do. Either vote for them or face certain doom.

In actuality, the Wannabe King usually has no clue about how to solve the problem, because it's a fantasy crisis. They may never have thought about it. To them, that's fine. Because *they don't actually care about the problem—the very problem they insist is ruining your life and putting the country in peril.* All they care about is winning and gaining power. We will look at several real-life examples of this in Part II of this book.

Choosing Targets of Blame

After the crisis is identified, the HCP chooses a villain—just the right target. Then, they publicly and relentlessly hammer that target with derision. A malignant narcissist—an HCP who is both a narcissist and a sociopath—has just the right combination of character traits to do this: a complete lack of empathy, ethics, and remorse; an overwhelming desire to dominate other people and be seen as extremely superior; a preoccupation with blaming others; and a sadistic pleasure in destroying their Targets of Blame.

Most of us don't strategically select our enemies; most of the time, Wannabe Kings do. Some do it quite consciously and deliberately; others do it reflexively and intuitively. But they always seem to use the same criteria.

A Wannabe King's villainous group needs to be

Somewhat familiar to voters so that the villains require no introduction or explanation.

Relatively few in number, or living elsewhere, or otherwise not part of most voters' daily lives, ensuring that most voters have little first-hand contact with members of the villainous group. They won't really know the reality of most group members' benign behavior.

Easy to define in a word or two, for example, Muslims, Jews, infidels, welfare queens, rich pigs, and so on. It makes no difference that it may be impossible to identify members of this villainous group on sight—or even after repeated contact.

Widely viewed as extremely powerful, when they are really weak, vulnerable, and a very small part of the population (typically only 1 to 3 percent) so that voters can hate them without much fear of retribution.

Already the target of some resentment, so that voters don't need too much training to hate them intensely.

If possible, resented because of their recent progress or achievement, which makes it possible for the Wannabe King to blame the fantasy crisis not just on the villains, but on those villains' *success.* This encourages voters to feel envious and angry as well as resentful.

Connected to money, finance, land, secret power or entertainment in some way, so the villainous group can be made to seem powerful and influential. If this connection can't be made, the Wannabe King typically cooks up a conspiracy theory that declares the group to be secretly ultra-powerful, despite their outward appearance as a vulnerable group.

Conclusion

Fantasy Crisis Triads created by Wannabe Kings are effective at escalating emotions so voters believe in their fantasy crises, which escalates their level of fear and emotional decision-making. Because of emotional repetition from the HCP, voters who dislike the fantasy hero have absorbed that the fantasy villain (the opposing candidate) is also so bad that they come to think of both of them as equally objectionable. In that case, Moderates tend to vote for their usual party's candidate, Resisters reject both opposing candidates by throwing away their votes on third-party candidates, and Dropouts simply don't vote.

All of this is assisted by the high-emotion media, which tend to favor HCPs, because they are more entertaining and put more energy into building an emotional relationship with their viewers and listeners. The result is that the emotional warfare of HCPs is endlessly repeated and they are often elected.

To counter this, we need to repeatedly ask ourselves—and encourage everyone we know to ask themselves—these three questions:

> *Is this really a crisis?*
>
> *Is this really a villain?*
>
> *Is this really a hero?*

In Part II we will see how the development of increasingly viral forms of high-emotion media has enabled HCP Wannabe Kings to promote their Fantasy Crisis Triads worldwide.

Part
II

THE FANTASY CRISIS TRIAD WORLDWIDE

The last one hundred years have been the most murderous in the history of humanity. I mentioned the top three perpetrators in Chapter 1: Hitler, Stalin, and Mao. However, many lesser Wannabe Kings have still destroyed their countries and killed hundreds of thousands of their countrymen. Although Hitler is often thought of as an exception, many of his strategies of extreme lying and conning appear to be templates for Wannabe Kings up to the present.

Since the year 2000, we have seen several Wannabe Kings take power around the world, including in Russia, Hungary, the Philippines, Venezuela, and Italy, as I will discuss in this part. The list keeps growing, so these are only a sample. The United States also has a substantial history of all sizes of Wannabe Kings, so I have chosen the three most dramatic examples: McCarthy, Nixon, and Trump.

All of these personalities sought unlimited power and relied heavily on numerous Fantasy Crisis Triads with shocking success. We must learn this pattern or we will keep repeating it.

HOW HITLER, STALIN, AND MAO TOOK OVER

These three Wannabe Kings all took power in the 1920s and 1930s after the monarchies of one form or another in their respective countries were eliminated. You might think that strong leaders would naturally follow such circumstances because the people were used to centralized governments, but the Wannabe Kings in the early twentieth century were far different. They each took a quantum leap in the mass manipulation of their people (via mass high-emotion media), they all desired and acquired unlimited power (as HCPs), and each brought horrific destruction to their countries and the world.

Adolf Hitler

Germany became a democracy immediately after World War I (WWI). Prior to that, it had been a monarchy, but in 1918, as Germany lost the war, the Kaiser abdicated the throne, and by default, the Social Democrats, the majority in the Kaiser's rubber-stamp Parliament, took power. The disarray after the war left an opening for an authoritarian government, but no one predicted an Adolf Hitler.

Hitler's Early Years

As described in Chapter 1, three basic factors influence how one's personality develops:

1. Genetic tendencies

2. Early childhood

3. Cultural environment

Adolf Hitler was born in Austria in 1889 to the family of a minor customs official on the border near Germany. On the surface, his childhood in Austria was not indicative of what he would become. Perhaps he was just born that way. We know he fought with his domineering father over his future career; his father wanted him to follow in his footsteps to become a civil servant, but young Hitler wanted to be a painter. When he was thirteen, his father died and his mother (who was reported to have had a loving relationship with Adolf) supported him and his sister on a meager pension.

> A boyhood friend later remembered him as a pale, sickly, lanky youth who, though usually shy and reticent, was capable of sudden bursts of hysterical anger against those who disagreed with him.[89]

He didn't leave much of an impression on his teachers, although one of his teachers later wrote this:

> Hitler was certainly gifted, although only for particular subjects, but he lacked self-control and, to say the least, he was considered argumentative, autocratic, self-opinionated and bad-tempered, and unable to submit to school discipline. Nor was he industrious; otherwise he would have achieved much better results, gifted as he was.[90]

When Hitler dropped out of high school, his mother continued to support him, although she encouraged him to get a career. Instead, he spent his time daydreaming, reading books, and becoming a young revolutionary. He had been inspired by one of his high school history teachers who was a fanatical German nationalist from southern Germany.[91]

As a young adult, Hitler wandered around Vienna, Austria, getting odd jobs as a laborer and making some small paintings for pay. He continued to read a lot and developed a reputation for being a bookish vagrant.[92] By twenty-four, he had no friends, no family, no job, and no home. However, he had "an unquenchable confidence in himself and a deep, burning sense of mission."[93]

Despite his air of confidence, he received more attention than he expected when, immediately after WWI, he began giving talks as "citizenship training" for army troops, in which he espoused his self-taught ideas of history, anti-Semitism, and future greatness for the German people.

> Hitler's skill and success were apparently a surprise even to him ... "I could speak!" he wrote, as though describing a Damascus Road experience.[94]

High-Conflict Personality

Hitler quickly adopted many people as his Targets of Blame. In his master text, *Mein Kampf* (which translates to *My Struggle*), he makes a lot out of a few negative encounters he had with Jews in Vienna as being the basis for his intense anti-Semitism. Some historians are skeptical about this, for example:

> In their view, Hitler's elaborate description of his politicization during his Vienna period was fabricated to fit the invented image of a naïve young man reacting to real conditions, not the reality of an aimless war veteran looking for work as a politician. In this interpretation, Hitler only seized on anti-Semitism "as the winning horse in the existing political environment," notes historian Roman Toppel.[95]

If he had a sociopathic personality, the roots of his anti-Semitism wouldn't really matter. He would have had an innate drive to dominate other people, especially those who were in a weaker position. By early adulthood, it already seemed clear that he had narcissistic personality traits; even he admitted that he was extremely self-absorbed and confident—even as a child. And Erich Fromm identified him as a malignant narcissist as well, as described in Chapter 1.

The Fantasy Crisis

Hitler used several fantasy crises as he rose to power. He easily hijacked the issue of criticizing the government in Berlin in the 1920s. More than anyone else, he passionately blamed the "traitors" at home (the Social Democrats in Berlin) for the loss of WWI. He spread false stories of the government stopping the generals from winning the war, when in fact the generals told the government that it could not be won. In November 1918, the leader of the German army High Command and his superior, Field Marshall von

Hindenburg, told Kaiser Wilhelm II that they had militarily lost the war and needed to stop fighting.[96]

In his speeches, Hitler promoted a new legend. The "November Criminals" (the Social Democrats signed the armistice in November), he cried, were responsible for the loss of the war, and the German army was "stabbed in the back." After the war, while the government was fanning the flames of hatred for France, Hitler had a different strategy in mind.

> The French occupation of the Ruhr, though it brought a renewal of German hatred for the traditional enemy and thus revived the spirit of nationalism, complicated Hitler's task. It began to unify the German people behind the republican government in Berlin which had chosen to defy France. This was the last thing Hitler wanted. His aim was to do away with the Republic. France could be taken care of after Germany had had its nationalist revolution and established a dictatorship. Against a strong current of public opinion Hitler dared to take an unpopular line: "No—not down with France, but down with the traitors of the Fatherland, down with the November criminals! That must be our slogan."[97]

By attacking targets *within* the country, he demonstrated this key characteristic of HCPs, which is to attack the people closest to you with emotional warfare in order to gain power over them.

The Fantasy Villains

Of course, Hitler more specifically blamed the defeat on the Jews, who he falsely claimed were in charge of the finance and production of the war. Soon, he began to blame everything that was wrong in Germany on the Jews, even though Jews made up less than 1 percent of the German population in the 1920s and 1930s (about 500,000 in a country of 67 million people).[98]

As Hitler began his rise to power, German Jews had only recently become accepted into mainstream society, and even then, they primarily lived in big cities such as Berlin. The great majority of Germans, especially in rural areas, did not know even one person who was Jewish. They readily believed whatever Hitler told them about Jews, since they knew no one who could verify or dispute Hitler's claims—and the media (radio and movies) were totally under his control.

This was, of course, an opportune time for Hitler to teach Germans to be intensely resentful of the Jews. After World War I, Germany struggled financially, and then the Great Depression started worldwide in 1929, at which point Germans faced increased unemployment, financial insecurity, and social and political instability.

Some think that until Hitler fanned these flames of resentment, the German people might have been only mildly anti-Semitic, and that the typical Nazi was not "specifically anti-Semitic," as described in Chapter 1. However, other historians believe that he simply took advantage of the virulent anti-Semitism that already existed.[99] We will never know.

But, as Dorothy Thompson, one of the most famous American journalists of the time, wrote after she interviewed Hitler and read *Mein Kampf*, "The Jews are responsible for everything...[T]ake the Jews out of Hitler's program, and the whole thing...collapses."[100]

In 1925, Hitler's *Mein Kampf* was published. It quickly proved popular and made Hitler a millionaire. By the end of the 1920s, he was getting more and more attention. At the time, he played up his anti-Communist rhetoric and played down his anti-Semitism to the American journalists, who he spoke to regularly and who took a keen interest in him. He was very deceptive about his ambitions:

> Instead of clarifying what he was for, Hitler dwelled on what he was against, including the Jews who had attained, as he put it, wildly disproportionate power and influence. "I am not for curtailing the rights of the Jews in Germany, but I insist that we **others who are not Jews shall not have less rights** than they," he said.[101] (emphasis added)

In this way, Hitler cleverly disguised what he was doing and eased the German people into resenting the "power and influence" of the Jews, rather than openly teaching hatred. They could deny being prejudiced at all. We will see this tactic used again and again by the other Wannabe Kings throughout Part II of this book.

He perfectly positioned himself to split the voters into four groups (see Chapter 3) by recruiting many people from the Disenchanted Dropouts to become Loving Loyalists, while he attacked both the Social Democrats (Moderates) and the Communists (Resisters) as villains because they were somehow both controlled by the Jews. He would be the new hero.

The Fantasy Hero

Hitler openly taught the German people that the democratic government was swindling them and that they would be better off with a dictatorship. But after 1924, which he spent in prison for trying to start a revolution at a beer hall (known as the Beer Hall Putsch), he decided to try to get elected to power:

> No longer was there to be a march on Berlin. The people were to "awaken" and Hitler's movement was going to *vote* dictatorship in! In itself a fascinating idea. Imagine a would-be dictator setting out *to persuade a sovereign people to vote away their rights.*[102] (Italics in original)

In 1933, after President Hindenburg appointed Hitler as chancellor, because he was head of the largest party, some of those in government believed that they could control him. One even declared "We've hired Hitler."[103]

A month after he was appointed chancellor, a small, easily contained fire broke out in the Reichstag (parliament) building. It was the act of a single mentally ill man from Holland who had been a member of a Communist youth group. Hitler claimed this incident (forever after known as the "Reichstag fire") was a Communist attempt to destroy parliament. [104]

This fantasy crisis enabled him to become the fantasy hero and allowed him to convince lawmakers to give him full legislative power. From then on, Hitler was able to make all of Germany's laws and rules. Six months later, Hindenburg died and Hitler assumed the post of president as well, claiming that he needed all political and military powers, allegedly because there was a (fantasy) plot against him, which "nobody believes" according to an American reporter in Berlin.[105]

High-Emotion Media

The Nazis, and especially Hitler, spoke publicly *ten times* as often as all other German politicians.[106] On a regular basis, Hitler spoke on the radio directly to citizens in their homes. In these speeches, he argued openly that what Germany most needed was a strong dictator, not a democracy.

He had movies made of his large rallies, which showed how powerful he was and how thousands of people deferred to him. Then he had these films shown in theaters throughout Germany.

🜲 🜲 🜲

Josef Stalin

Russia was firmly ruled by the Romanov Tsars until the communist revolution of February 1917. Tsar Nicholas II abdicated his throne in the face of widespread protests and violence driven by major losses in World War I and widespread hunger. A broad provisional government took over, endorsing numerous liberal reforms, including freedom of speech and assembly. This government set elections for a broad constituent assembly in October 1917 to represent every citizen, regardless of class, which would have included all revolutionary parties, urban and rural. [107]

But it was a chaotic year, and before the October elections could take place, Vladimir Lenin's tightly-run Bolshevik Party of urban workers, sailors, and soldiers stormed the Winter Palace in St. Petersburg, the seat of the Russian Provisional Government. They arrested government ministers as betraying the revolution, but members of the legislature walked out in protest and the civil service, post office, and banks went on strike. Regardless, the end result is that the Bolsheviks were in charge of St. Petersburg.

When the election for the constituent assembly came, the Bolsheviks only won 24 percent of the vote. But because they were the most centrally organized party and had the strength of the workers and military in Moscow and St. Petersburg, they shut down the constituent assembly after only one day and took total control of the whole government, establishing a Congress of Soviets that they said was superior to the constituent assembly. This is known as the *Bolshevik Coup* or the *October Revolution*.

Stalin's Early Years

Josef Stalin was born in 1878 in Georgia, a recent addition to the Russian empire at that time.[108] His father was a notorious drunk and gave young Stalin many undeserved beatings. One boyhood friend said his father made Stalin learn to hate people. [109]

On the other hand, early on, his mother loved him and spoiled him, and she eventually became the mistress of another man who became a kinder substitute father.[110] But as he grew up, Stalin became so hard to control that his mother also ended up beating him, which helped him cement his belief in violence as being the way to manage relationships.[111]

But during this childhood, Stalin loved to study books and his mother sensed that he was gifted.[112] He also enjoyed hanging out in his neighborhood during this time, which was one of the roughest places in Georgia, on the edge of Russia.

> Gori was one of the last towns to practice the "picturesque and savage custom" of free-for-all town brawls with special rules but no-holds-barred violence. . . . The saloon-bars of Gori were incorrigible stews of violence and crime. . . .[113]

Psychological historians attribute much of Stalin's development to his drunken father, but learning to become skilled as a fighter in this street fighting culture probably played an important role as well.[114]

As an adult, after many false starts—including a stint at a seminary—Stalin became involved in revolutionary politics and joined the Communist Party. He was especially regarded for his knowledge of Marxist writing and theory. Stalin played a lesser role in the Bolshevik's Communist Party, essentially missing both revolutions, which he was constantly reminded of by his peers. [115]

By March 1922, Lenin named Stalin the General Secretary of the Communist Party, an administrative position created for him, as he showed promise with bureaucratic skills. In April, at the Central Committee congress, Lenin

> "organized a conspiratorial meeting in a side room, gathering his most reliable followers, 27 people, to ensure election to the Central Committee of his preferred candidates against Trotsky's followers; Stalin's name was marked on Lenin's list as "general secretary . . . ." All 27 names on Lenin's list were duly elected . . .[116]

When the vote was taken at the congress, Stalin received "193 votes in favor, 16 against; the rest (273), more than half the voting delegates, effectively abstained." This means he got 40 percent of the vote—the consistent percentage of all of our Wannabe Kings. It is notable that the collective leadership "couldn't see whom they were dealing with."[117]

High-Conflict Personality

Stalin always had an intense drive to dominate:

> He was ruthless to other children, but protective of his vassals. . . . Stalin constantly defied lads "older and stronger than himself."

> He displayed the will to power that remained with him until his last days. "Soso [his nickname at the time] belonged to his local gang but he often crossed to the opposing band because he refused to obey his own gangleader . . . he developed a vengeful feeling against everyone positioned above himself." As soon as he was out of his mother's control, Stalin, even as a child, had to be the leader.[118]

That Stalin had a high-conflict personality from early childhood seems quite clear—much clearer than Hitler. He also had the extreme aggressiveness that could not be contained by anyone, even his mother, from boyhood on. His ruthlessness fits well with the characteristics of a sociopath, and that he had a narcissistic personality may have been demonstrated early on with his "infectious confidence" that made people want to follow him.[119]

Even though his position as General Secretary was a purely administrative post, he used his aggressive personality and administrative skills to transform his role into that of the Communist Party's leader after Lenin died in 1924. By 1929, he had seized all power. He was the Soviet Union's all-powerful dictator until his death in 1953.

The Fantasy Crisis

Stalin imagined many crises and created many crises. The solution he offered for each crisis was to brutally attack one group of people (his Targets of Blame) while convincing the other Soviet citizens to trust and invest unlimited power in him.

As briefly described in Chapter 2, the most dramatic example of his brutality was the famines caused by his policy of collectivizing the peasants' farms throughout the Soviet Union, including Russia and Ukraine. In the early years after the revolution, the peasants in the countryside (who had been subjugated and brutalized for hundreds of years before the Tsarist system fell) had run the landed gentry off their land and divided it up among themselves. They had become owners of their own small plots of land. They made their own decisions about what to grow and how to spend their own small funds. However, since those early years, the Communist government had come to dominate them.

By 1927, the Communist government had not brought better times to the workers and the peasants. "[L]iving standards in the Soviet Union were still lower than they had been under the tsars."[120] The government had manipulated theoretically free market prices (industrial goods were set high and agricultural products were set low), which had thrown off incentives for farmers so that there were mounting shortages of food, especially grain, and skyrocketing "private" prices.

Rather than blame these shortages of food on terrible government policies, he treated this as a fantasy crisis with fantasy villains.

But by 1931, Stalin envisioned an even bigger crisis.

> He believed that another European war was coming, and that, in order to survive it, backward Russia would have to industrialize. "We are fifty to a hundred years behind the advanced countries," he declared in 1931. "We must make good this gap in ten years. Either we do it, or they will crush us."

Rapid industrialization would require that peasants deliver grain to the state on a set schedule; it would also require that many peasants become industrial workers. The U.S.S.R. needed large, mechanized farms, like those in the United States. And the independent, landowning peasantry was a threat.[121]

Fantasy Villains

As explained in Chapter 2, *kulaks* was the term used for peasant farmers who had slightly more than the poorer peasants. Stalin made them into the villains.

"Either we destroy the kulaks as a class," Stalin said in 1929, using the term for rich or greedy ("fist-like") peasants, "or the kulaks will grow as a class of capitalists and liquidate the dictatorship of the proletariat."[122]

The only solution, Stalin insisted, was to murder or exile this entire class of people. State police shot and killed hundreds of thousands of kulaks; hundreds of thousands more were deported. With most of the kulaks gone, Stalin and the Soviet government were able to seize control of the country's agriculture. They then used the capital extracted from the countryside to build manufacturing.

Stalin also frequently blamed crises on "enemies of the people." This phrase, which he repeated often, allowed each Russian to heartily agree with Stalin, based on whatever group that person hated.

The Fantasy Hero

During World War II, Stalin was caught by surprise when Hitler invaded Russia in 1941. The Soviet dictator had assumed that he and Hitler were friends, as they had even discussed going to war together in Europe. So he ignored all the warnings, even those from Britain and the US.[123] Yet, even so, Stalin somehow marshalled his troops and beat back the Germans, but at a terrible loss of life to the Soviet people.

Over the course of his rule, Stalin caused the deaths of approximately 20 million civilians within the Soviet Union.[124] Yet enormous numbers of Soviet citizens loved him, cheered him on, and felt that he was an ideal leader. He had the classic "cult of personality" that is associated with aggressive Wannabe Kings.

High-Emotion Media

No one could escape Stalin's domineering presence in photos and on the radio throughout the Soviet Union. With total control of the media, his emotional repetition was powerful—and in isolation, increasing its power as I described in Chapter 4. The idea of the Iron Curtain around the Soviet Union and its satellites included keeping out all outside competing opinions. He was a prolific writer and loved to give speeches.

♟ ♟ ♟

Mao Zedong

China was ruled by emperors for almost two thousand years, ending with the nearly 300-year Qing dynasty (also known as the Manchu dynasty). After years of unrest, famine, and corruption, it was overthrown by a revolution and the establishment of the Republic of China in 1912. After a series of military leaders and instability, a nationalist government was established by Chiang Kai-shek in 1928. The country had no real history of democracy and elections, so change and revolutionary fervor were in the air. The Communist Party of China was new in the 1920s and opposed the nationalist government.[125]

Mao's Early Years

Mao Zedong was born in 1893. He had an easy childhood. His father worked hard as a farmer and was thrifty, so he became one of the most well-to-do peasants in their village. Mao was loved and indulged by his mother and grandmother. He loved learning, had an excellent memory, and had a passion for reading. However, he also was headstrong and disobedient, which resulted in him having clashes with his teachers and getting kicked out of three schools.[126]

Mao's father expected him to help with farm work, but Mao hated physical labor. He also hated his father. After years of conflict, his father was looking for a way to settle Mao down. He decided to arrange a marriage to his niece when Mao was fourteen and she was eighteen. He was obviously hoping Mao's new wife would take Mao to task. It was not to be so, though. Mao ignored her and became opposed to arranged marriages.[127]

When Mao's wife died two years later, his father let him leave the village to go to a modern school in the city. There he learned about the world, went to a teacher-training college, and later became a young Communist leader. The Communist Party was being formed and funded in China by Stalin's Soviet Union.[128]

High-Conflict Personality

Mao's writings as a young adult revealed an extremely self-centered and hedonistic man.

> "People like me want to . . . satisfy our hearts to the full, and in doing so we automatically have the most valuable moral codes. Of course there are people and objects in the world, but they are all there only for me."
>
> Mao shunned all constraints of responsibility and duty. "People like me only have a duty to ourselves; we have no duty to other people."
>
> . . .
>
> Mao did not believe in anything unless he could benefit from it personally.[129]

Like Hitler, he saw himself as a great hero who would have great powers:

> When Great Heroes give full play to their impulses, they are magnificently powerful, stormy and invincible. Their power is like a hurricane arising from a deep gorge, and like a sex-maniac on heat and prowling for a lover . . . there is no way to stop them.[130]

These descriptions certainly suggest both a narcissistic personality and a sociopathic personality, or malignant narcissism with fantasies of unlimited power.

The Communist Party in China was started and funded by Stalin and the leadership of the Soviet Union in Moscow in an effort to expand their influence. Mao missed the founding Party Congress, but he was in the immediate outer ring of the party and was given the job of running a bookstore to sell party literature.[131]

Mao was extremely ambitious and skilled at manipulating and attacking his colleagues and those above him over the years, and he did so in order to gain power. He rapidly formed and dispensed with alliances in the Communist Party and eventually in the Red Army. He was a party official in the Red Army's Long March across China in their retreat from fighting for power against the Chinese Nationalist Army of the government. Rather than having to march, he and some other officials were carried in litters.[132]

In January 1935, the march stopped for a leadership meeting in Zunyi to decide what to do after some important military losses.

> Mao had started taking active steps to seize the leadership of his Party once the marchers entered Guizhou. **This required splitting his Party foes from within.** In particular, he had been cultivating two key men with

whom he had not previously been on the best terms... Mao had crossed swords with them in the past, but **now he buttered them up**, as they both had grudges against Party No. 1 Po Ku.[133] (Emphasis added)

During this meeting, the leadership rehashed who was responsible for these military failures. Mao and his two allies strongly criticized the key leaders from before the Long March. In the process, Mao became a member of the Secretariat, the decision-making core. Although it was untrue, he spread the claim that he had become the leader of the Party and the army at this meeting—by majority mandate. In fact, he was never elected to either role.He was just elected to be one member of the Secretariat.[134]

He was endlessly aggressive and blaming, without any empathy or remorse in his drive for personal power. It appears, as in the following quote, that everyone else around him had a sense of restraint that allowed Mao to run them over, since he had none.

With his back to the wall, Mao fought with fearsome willpower and enormous rage, condemning Peng with political labels like "right-wing," and accusing him of stirring up Lin Biao. When Lin tried to reason, Mao just bellowed: "You are a baby! You don't know a thing!" Lin could not compete with Mao in a shouting match, and was bludgeoned into silence. Peng was doomed by his own decency and decorum. Unlike Mao, he was shy about fighting for power for himself, even though his cause was good. Nor could he match Mao in mudslinging and "political" smearing.[135]

One skill Mao had was spreading false information about his power, as he did with the claim of being the party's and army's leader. For example, after leading his troops into suicidal battles losing some 30,000 men, he "shamelessly called this his 'tour de force.'"[136] This misinformation worked for him, because when he met up with a more powerful division, he was given a top military job.

He then sent an envoy to Moscow to establish his authority; they misrepresented that Mao had been elected party chief at the meeting in Zunyi. Moscow then appointed Mao chairman of the Central Executive Committee. Thus, he became Chairman Mao, a title for him that would become world famous. In other words, Mao was never elected to his top position, but rather he created and promoted this myth throughout his lifetime.[137]

The Fantasy Crisis

Mao ruled ruthlessly and took a similar approach to Communism that Stalin took: *I'm in charge and whatever I do is good for the people.* Thus, collectivization was the cure for all ills. One of his fantasy crises was the Great Leap Forward. It was necessary to catch up to the rest of the modern world, otherwise they were at risk.

> In 1958 he had a revelation that the country could double its steel pro-duction in a year if peasant families contributed to the national output by running backyard smelters. . . . It was also revealed to him that China could grow large quantities of grain on small plots of land, freeing the rest for grasslands and gardens. . . . Peasants were herded into communes of 50,000 to implement this vision, and anyone who dragged his feet or pointed out the obvious was executed as a class enemy.[138]

The Fantasy Villains

During the Great Leap Forward, anyone who resisted in any way or didn't meet quotas was considered an enemy. As with Stalin, peasants who didn't cooperate were Targets of Blame with terrible consequences; millions died.

In his next Fantasy Crisis, the villains were almost anyone who *wasn't* a peasant. Less than ten years after the disaster of the Great Leap Forward, Mao had another inspiration:

> During the Cultural Revolution of 1966–75, Mao encouraged maraud-ing Red Guards to terrorize "class enemies," including teachers, manag-ers, and the descendants of landlords and "rich peasants," killing perhaps 7 million.[139]

The Fantasy Hero

Just as with Hitler and Stalin, Mao had quite an emotional mass following who treated him as a god. By having his endless speeches blared from public speakers in town and urban squares, and by having his photo plastered everywhere, Mao was able to keep the people seduced with emotional repe-tition in isolation; they had only his messages to hear.

Despite his disastrous policies, his propaganda efforts promoting him-self were extremely successful. During the Cultural Revolution in 1966,

> . . . the cult of Mao was escalated to fever pitch. Mao's face dominated the front page of *People's Daily*, which also ran a column of his quotations every day. Soon, badges started appearing with Mao's head on them, of which, altogether, some 4.8 billion were manufactured. More copies of Mao's *Selected Works* were printed—and more portraits of him (1.2 billion)—than China had inhabitants. It was this summer that the Little Red Book

was handed out to everyone. It had to be carried and brandished on all public occasions, and its prescriptions recited daily.[140]

High-Emotion Media

We have already seen how Mao's face was everywhere. His Little Red Book of sayings was everywhere. During the Cultural Revolution, he had students everywhere publicly condemning their teachers on the radio and from loudspeakers "rigged up everywhere, creating an atmosphere that was both blood-boiling and blood-curdling."[141]

His successful myth-making has left a lasting heritage. Multitudes attended his funeral, and his body and picture still remain on display in Tiananmen Square in Beijing to this day.[142]

Conclusion

In all three of these examples, we have individuals who had similar and extreme patterns of emotional warfare and Fantasy Crisis Triads. Warning signs of their unrestrained personality patterns were evident early on in their political careers, but most people didn't know what to look for and didn't realize the danger they posed until it was too late.

Politically, Stalin and Mao were far to the left, and Hitler was far to the right. Remember, it's not about the politics, it's about the personalities. Now we'll look at a sampling of current Wannabe Kings around the world and how they got elected.

AROUND THE WORLD TODAY: RUSSIA, HUNGARY, THE PHILIPPINES, VENEZUELA, AND ITALY

In elections since 2000, several nations have chosen leaders who have viciously attacked fantasy villains within their own countries and structurally attacked their own democratic procedures. They exhibit the same patterns of HCP Wannabe Kings as the historical leaders in the prior chapter. Although current HCPs have more restraints in place at the moment, they also have much more potential technological power to be dangerous and much more power to be deceptive using the latest high-emotion media. To date, their successes at creating and exaggerating fantasy crises has been stunning.

Russia: Vladimir Putin

In 1991, the Soviet Union ceased to exist. Boris Yeltsin took over as the president of Russia and essentially took control of what was left of the institutions of the central Soviet government, which were always based in Russia.

Over the next several years, there was a drive toward a market economy, free speech, and democratic elections, but by 1999, this all slowed when the world economic crisis hit Russia hard. Boris Yeltsin was wearing out physically and mentally and he appointed Vladimir Putin to replace himself as president.

Putin's Early Years

Vladimir Putin was born in 1952. His mother worked as a cleaning woman but doted on him because his older brothers had both died young. His father was a factory worker and a representative in the Communist Party. He grew up poor and was highly disruptive in and out of school. Putin "was once rebuked for delinquency by a neighborhood [Communist] party committee, which threatened to send him to an orphanage."[143]

He did not join the Pioneers, the Communist Party's youth group, when he was very young. "I was a hooligan, not a Pioneer," he once said.[144] But then he took up martial arts, enjoying its strict discipline.

> The martial arts transformed his life, giving him the means of asserting himself against larger, tougher boys. . . . The martial arts gave him an orthodoxy he found neither in religion nor in politics. It was more than mere sport, he believed; it was a philosophy.[145]

His commitment to martial arts eventually led him to join the Pioneers and become the leader of his school's branch. Then, in eighth grade, he joined the Communist Party's youth organization, Komsomol. He was well on his way to his life's work.

High-Conflict Personality

In his youth, Putin saw a movie about a KGB secret agent and impulsively decided that was what he wanted to become. He liked the idea that one person could affect the lives of thousands.[146]

By the time Yeltsin appointed him to be the next president, he was head of the KGB. At the time, the economic crisis was hitting the country hard. No one expected him to last long.

> [By then, most Russians] wanted a savior, a leader who would be not merely decisive but dominating. Putin hardly seemed suited for that role: he had no history and no presence.[147]

But from August to November 1999, based on his tough talk and aggressive actions (described next), independent polls went from a 31-percent to an 80-percent belief that he was doing "a good job."[148]

Fantasy Crisis

When Putin took office as president, he restarted the war on Chechnya. Apparently, this played well with the Russian people, because he seemed to be acting and sounding like a leader—and he seemed stronger and more determined than Yeltsin.

Fantasy Villains

Putin termed the Chechen rebels terrorists.

> "We will pursue terrorists wherever they are. At the airport, if they are at the airport. And that means, I apologize, that if we catch them going to the bathroom, then we will rub them out in the outhouse, if it comes to that. That's it, the issue is closed." [149]

A majority of people liked his tough way of speaking and were charmed by his appearance of strength, modesty, and reason. He seemed to be a leader, but at the same time a man of the people.

When United States Ambassador Michael McFaul arrived in Russia in January, 2012, he was immediately targeted by Putin as an agent who had come to Russia to foment revolution—a claim purposefully made to help Putin in the run-up to his March election. In February, a video came out falsely suggesting that McFaul was a pedophile, which went viral, since numerous politicians in Russia were also being accused of pedophilia with no basis in reality. The Russian government was believed to be behind the attacks.[150]

Such treatment of an ambassador was previously unheard of. These false claims were the tactics Putin used against Russian critics and now his biggest Targets of Blame: the United States and its representative in Moscow.

Fantasy Hero

Surveys in 1999 showed that the Russian people were nostalgic for the old Soviet Union days: 58 percent said they would prefer the way things were before 1985, 26 percent said that Stalin's rule had been good for the country (compared to 18 percent in 1994), and a majority no longer held a negative view of the old dictator.[151]

The fantasy hero to lead Russia was back, in the form of Vladimir Putin. But would he be a strong democratic leader, or would he try to return the nation to a totalitarian form of government?

[By 2002] in just two years, Putin had greatly weakened the power of elected officials by creating federal oversight over governors and giving the federal center the right to fire elected governors; reversed judicial reform; and monopolized national broadcast television in the hands of the Kremlin. So while his regime could not yet be called authoritarian, that seemed to be the direction in which it was headed. This transitional state . . . was . . . an "authoritarian situation"—meaning, authoritarianism could happen here.[152]

Although Putin had a domineering personality, he also seemed to have narcissistic aspects. It was said that "The new president was getting a reputation for being thin-skinned and vengeful. . . ."[153]

The Russian constitution sets no limits on how many years someone can hold the office of president. It merely forbids a president from serving more than two *consecutive* terms. Putin served two such terms from 2000 through 2008. He was succeeded by Dmitri Medvedev, who immediately appointed Putin prime minister.

At the end of Medvedev's term, Putin decided to run again for president. By November 2011, polls showed that he had only 34-percent support from likely voters. After he announced he would run again, many people were outraged. In December 2011, his party (United Russia) did poorly compared to expectations in the parliamentary elections but they still somehow won the most votes. Clear evidence that the election had been manipulated brought hundreds of thousands into the streets, more than at any time since the Soviet Union collapse in 1991.

Putin's first reaction to these Russian demonstrators was anger. In his mind, he had made these young professionals rich, and now they had turned against him. Even his former finance minister, Alexei Kudrin, attended one of these demonstrations. That was betrayal. Putin's second reaction was fear. He and his team were surprised by the size of the protests. Never before had so many Russians demonstrated against his rule. The message from the streets quickly turned radical, starting with outrage against falsification, but morphing into demands for the end of Putin's regime. [154]

So Putin decided to use Hillary Clinton and George Soros, in addition to McFaul, as his targets in the lead-up to the March 2012 election. At the time, even Russian President Medvedev personally told McFaul that things would calm down after the election.[155] But as we have seen before, such tactics work; Putin went on from only 34-percent support in December to win the election in March. Then he cracked down further on dissent.[156]

High-Emotion Media

From his first year as president in 2000, Putin has been building his authoritarian rule by dominating the media. "Putin had acquired de facto control of Russia's three largest and most important television channels before the end of his first year in office."[157]

No meaningful competitors have come up with alternatives to the messages he wants to give to the nation. Over the years he has made claims of a "pedophile menace," "propaganda of homosexuality," and the West's "attack" on Russia's Christian values and traditions. After so many years of promoting his various fantasy crises on television, he had the majority of the country behind him in 2012. They knew who their (fantasy) villains were and, certainly, who their (fantasy) hero was. He taught them well.

When the 2018 elections came around, everyone knew that Putin would win since no serious opponents were allowed on the ballot. Just prior to that election, the *New York Times* ran a story about Putin's support among women in Russia and the role that his use of television has with them.

> The special relationship between Russian women and Vladimir Putin goes back to the very beginning of his years in power. In the 2000 elections—the first time Mr. Putin's name was on the ballot—61 percent of his votes came from women and just 39 percent from men. . . . In 2012, 75 percent of women offered a favorable opinion of Mr. Putin, compared with 69 percent of men, according to the Pew Research Center. . . .
>
> Older women are a particular bastion of support. I spent a week in St. Petersburg last month and spoke to a dozen older women from different walks of life, with a variety of income and educational levels. All told me they were voting for him. Most said they were doing so in part **because he was a good man—strong, healthy and active. . . .**
>
> . . . By the time women reach retirement age, their husbands have often died, and their days consist of taking care of grandchildren, spending time with other older women and **watching television**.[158] (Emphasis added)

Vladimir Putin appears to be a classic example of a Wannabe King. Once again, a single person's personality has made a world of difference and has ended his nation's fledgling democracy. This was not inevitable. Yeltsin almost appointed another man, Boris Nemtsov, in 1999.

> Yeltsin might have very well selected Nemtsov as his successor, and the world might never have heard of Vladimir Putin. . . . He had the skills and charisma to have become a successful president—a successful *democratic* president.[159] (Emphasis in original)

♔ ♔ ♔

Hungary: Viktor Orban

Hungary was one of the Warsaw Pact countries that came under the domination of the Soviet Union after World War II. It had a revolution the Soviet Union put down in 1956, although it eventually did gain more freedom from the Soviet Union than most Warsaw Pact nations. It wasn't until the Soviet Union started coming apart at the seams in 1989 that Hungary became an independent, democratic, parliamentary republic.

By 1990, Hungary held its first free parliamentary elections, and by 1991, all Soviet troops had left Hungary. In 1999, Hungary joined NATO, and in 2004, it joined the European Union. It was with these moves that it pulled free of Russia and tilted West with strong democratic ties to the United States and Europe. One of the young student leaders who formed a group to help launch the pro-democracy movement in the 1980s was Viktor Orban.

Orban's Early Years

Viktor Orban was born in 1963. He was a country boy who grew up in villages in Hungary where his father was an agronomist and entrepreneur and his mother was a speech therapist and special educator. He served two years in the military and then went to law school. To be admitted to law school, he was required to join the Communist youth group, so he did and became a leader.

In college, he later rejected Communism and the Communist government in Hungary. He helped form the pro-democracy group that later became the political party Fidesz. Where there were elections in 1990, his group won 22 seats in the government. But soon thereafter things changed.

> Within two years, however, a battle over Fidesz's soul would erupt that showed Orban's early willingness to change his political ideology in pursuit of power. As Hungary's first post-communist, centre-right government struggled against economic collapse, some of the party's co-founders wanted to ally with a bigger liberal party. Orban thought Fidesz would be swallowed up. He wanted to take the party to the right, where he thought it could become the dominant political force. "Orban said, 'Our main enemy is the liberal party. It's a fight, and we have to win,'" says Fodor.[160]

High-Conflict Personality

In 2010, Orban and his right-wing Fidesz party were elected to power and they have dominated Hungary ever since. In the past eight years, Orban has put significant effort into dismantling the democracy that elected him. He individually chose this direction, according to reports of a meeting that occurred in 2010.

> The senior leaders of Fidesz gathered on the banks of the Danube, in a building known as the Hungarian White House, stunned by the scale of their good fortune. Their right-wing party had won unexpectedly sweeping political power in national elections. The question was how to use it.
>
> Several men urged caution. But Viktor Orban, the prime minister-elect, disagreed. The voting result, Mr. Orban continued, had given him the right to carry out a radical overhaul of the country's Constitution.[161]

Since he came to power, he has aggressively moved to rewrite the Hungarian Constitution, impose restrictions on civil society, and divert European Union money and federal government money for his own purposes. He has put restrictions on the Hungarian media, has redrawn electoral maps to favor his party, and has sought to take control of the judiciary, which was overruling many of his authoritarian efforts.

Although Hungary was hailed as a democracy after it got out from under the Soviet Union in the 1990s, Orban has almost single-handedly created what he calls an "illiberal democracy." He has made Hungary appear to be a normal European country, while he has really turned it into a dictatorship.[162]

Fantasy Crises

Orban claims that Hungarians are victims who are being treated poorly by the European Union, by immigrants, and especially by George Soros, a Hungarian-born American.

Fantasy Villain

George Soros is a multibillionaire whose life story has a fascinating arc. As a young Jewish citizen of Hungary during World War II, he had the misfortune of being a prisoner at a concentration camp. He survived, and after the war, he moved to the United States and became a wildly successful investor in the stock market. He also invested in efforts to promote democracy in his old country and around the world.

Ironically, he has become the Target of Blame for Orban and Fidesz. Turning Soros into a villain helped Orban win a fourth term as president in March 2018.

> After the fall of the Berlin Wall, in 1989, [Soros] poured hundreds of millions of dollars into the former Soviet-bloc countries to promote civil society and

liberal democracy. It was a one-man Marshall Plan for Eastern Europe, a private initiative without historical precedent. . . .

He also finds himself in the unsettling position of being **the designated villain** of this anti-globalization backlash, his Judaism and career in finance rendering him a made-to-order phantasm for reactionaries worldwide.[163] (Emphasis added)

Fantasy Hero

Orban and his party are the fantasy heroes—and not just for Hungary.

With national variations, Mr. Orban's Hungary has been the template for the "authoritarianization"—the term some experts use—in Jaroslaw Kaczynski's Poland, Recep Tayyip Erdogan's Turkey, Vladimir Putin's Russia, and in other democracies where populism has made headway. . . . The populists, no matter how narrowly elected, assume that electoral victory was the will of the people and, in a terrible irony, a license to trample on the same democracy that raised them to power.[164]

Orban and his party are all over billboards, TV, and radio. Orban has gained much power in Hungary through these antidemocratic efforts, and the European Union has mostly been ineffective at stopping him. Although they hold the purse strings for a lot of funding that goes to Hungary, they don't want to upset the balance of power with the former Eastern European nations that have become EU members.[165]

High-Emotion Media

Orban used the immigration crisis of 2015 to get reelected in 2018, even though he and his government largely ended that problem three years earlier by placing severe restrictions on who can enter the country.

Immigration was a major focus of the [2018] election, and throughout the day, state television replayed some of the most dramatic images from 2015, when the crisis of refugees and immigrants flooding into Europe from the Middle East and Africa was at its peak.[166]

Fantasy crises can live on for years, when you control state television and the images it projects.

With his manipulation of the message and restrictions on the press, he has created the opportunity for his emotional repetition in isolation. Because the opposition is divided and because he has remapped electoral districts, he continues to control the government even though his party got fewer votes in the most recent election compared to prior years.

Once his party won two-thirds of the seats in Parliament in 2018, it was positioned to change the Constitution and do whatever it wished to "protect Hungary."[167]

w w w

The Philippines: Rodrigo Duterte

The Philippines is a nation of 7,000 islands in the South Pacific Ocean. The United States won control of the Philippines from Spain in 1898 at the end of the Spanish-American War. The US ruled the Philippines until it was captured by the Japanese during World War II, from 1942 to 1944; at that point, the US regained control. In 1946, however, the Philippines became an independent nation with a democratic constitution and elections. Since then, it has also grown rapidly; it had a population of 30 million in 1970 and at the time of this writing it is over 100 million.

Ferdinand Marcos dominated Filipino politics with martial law and an iron fist from 1965 to 1986, when he was ousted by the nonviolent "People Power" movement and fled the country. Thirty years of democratic elections followed before Rodrigo Duterte came to power.[168]

Duterte's Early Years

Rodrigo Duterte was born in 1945. His father was a lawyer and his mother was a school teacher. They both became involved in politics, his father as a mayor and then a governor. By high school, Duterte had been kicked out of two schools for "unruly behavior," but he ultimately finished at a Catholic high school.

> It was not that he was a bad student. He just enjoyed hanging around with city toughs and became street-smart, picking up their vocabulary and mannerism. Although it caused immense trouble during his school days and earned him severe whipping at home, the experience later helped him to connect with the masses.[169]

He subsequently went to law school and became first a prosecutor in Davao City and then its mayor in 1988. He spent most of the next twenty years in that office, except for a few years as a congressman from 1998 to 2001.[170]

High-Conflict Personality

Duterte's success in ruling Davao may give some indications about his personality. Between 1998 and 2016, death squads in Davao were alleged to have executed over 1,400 people. Duterte has alternately confirmed and denied his involvement in these death squads, but we do know that throughout this time, he held widespread support.

> Over two decades, at a time when Davao was doubling in size to over 1.5 million, Duterte transformed the city from a Third World hellhole into a pleasant place for a law-abiding person to live—even a business hub. He pulled this off by mixing wiles and ruthlessness, offering Muslims and Communists financial incentives to carry their campaigns elsewhere and threatening them with retribution should they not. Many human rights groups hold him responsible for about 1,000 unsolved killings during his tenure, carried out by shadowy assailants who came to be called the Davao Death Squad.[171]

In 2016, Duterte was elected President of the Philippines, in part because of his promises to rein in drug trafficking and to reduce the extreme poverty of many in the country. Duterte was able to pull together a coalition of conservative Filipinos, overseas labor migrants, members of the educated middle class, urban poor, and informal workers to be elected president.

For his first two years, he maintained a steady approval rating of around 80 percent. His pursuit of his drug war has been a big part of that; it has over 70 percent approval.[172]

Fantasy Crisis

Duterte has used strong, violent language about the drug problem in the Philippines, but there are questions about the actual size of this problem. It is not clear that Filipinos actually see drug use as a crisis. A respected poll every year of the five most concerning problems has never had drug use make the list. People are concerned about drug dealers, but they would rather suspects be caught alive and prosecuted than shot down in cold blood in the streets by unidentifiable marauders on motorcycles (who many believe are actually police).[173]

Fantasy Villains

Are the villains just drug dealers, or are all drug addicts villains in Duterte's mind? He claims that addicts often become dealers, which gives his war a much wider reach and could allow the killing of just about anyone.

Small-time users, not just big-time pushers, are targets for aggressive police operations. A bloodbath has resulted. Last August, the government's "One-Time Bigtime" busts left 52 dead in one night. By the turn of this year, 4,075 people had died in anti-drug operations, according to the government. . . . Whether the killers are out-of-uniform policemen silencing witnesses to their own corruption or neighborhood hoodlums using the drug war as a cover to settle scores, the violence has been immense.[174]

Fantasy Heroes

Duterte has been viewed as a hero by a large number of Filipinos. The police are also frequently seen as heroes, but they too may be part of the fantasy. They are frequently identified as corrupt and a *source* of drugs. They often collect money from the funeral parlors that get the bodies of those they have killed. Ironically, police violence and corruption may be the biggest barriers to reducing the drug problem.[175]

Occasionally, Duterte accuses the police of corruption, but this doesn't last. One theory is that his true goal with the extreme police measures he has advocated in his drug war is to lay the groundwork for establishing an authoritarian government with himself as dictator.[176]

But will the Filipino people put up with a dictatorial approach? Some think that the Philippine population places a deep value on loyalty and deference. However, depending on the circumstances, this loyalty can easily and suddenly change.

This is a democracy that social conventions render capable of behaving like an autocracy. Representatives can turn like a school of fish.[177]

High-Conflict Media

As with all of the other Wannabe Kings, Duterte is constantly giving speeches and talking to the people on television, emotionally repeating the same messages of victimhood and the evil people behind it.

But it's not just what he says and how he says it on the media. Signs are pointing to Duterte also gaining control of the media so that his emotionally repetitive messages may also become in isolation for his people, making the messages all the more powerful. He threatened the owners of the country's top newspaper and top online news source with jail unless they sold their interest to a close Duterte supporter. They did.

Duterte was also the first politician in the Philippines to master the use of social media in an election, and he used it a lot in 2016, including fake news posts.

> ("Even the Pope admires Duterte," ran one quite false post.) Today, many of the country's top bloggers are Duterte diehards, like the "30-ish-year-old Filipino citizen journalist" R. J. Nieto, who blogs under the name Thinking Pinoy (the Filipino word for Filipino) and describes himself as "crazily patriotic, almost a nut job." Nieto is described by his adversaries as one of the worst practitioners of "fake news."[178]

♛ ♛ ♛

Venezuela: Nicolas Maduro

Venezuela is an oil-rich nation that had a democracy for many years. It was seen as a success story among the world's developing nations. Although it was dominated by an oligarchy of wealthy families and most people remained very poor, there was a growing middle class.[179]

In 1998, Hugo Chavez was elected president with 56 percent of the vote, with his closest opponent garnering only 39 percent. He did not have any prior experience as a politician and had not even worked in the public sector prior to his election. He saw himself as the leader of a revolution. His goals were to end corruption, democratize the oil industry, and end poverty. He was a charismatic leader, fighting for the poor against the rich and against the United States, which he regularly blasted in his television speeches.

However, Chavez is not the focus here. He died of cancer in 2013 and Venezuelans went on to elect his hand-picked successor, Nicolas Maduro, by a very slim majority.

Maduro's Early Years

As a youth, Maduro claims he was a bit of a hippie. He rode (and crashed) motorcycles, played in a band, and studied the teachings of an Indian mystic. In politics, however, Maduro was more hard-nosed. His father had been a leftist trade unionist, and, at the age of twelve, Maduro joined the student union, where he became known as an outspoken partisan. He dropped out of school soon afterward and later joined the leftist group the Socialist League, whose slogan was "Socialism is won by fighting."[180]

High-Conflict Personality

Maduro lacked the charisma of Chavez and the money of the Venezuelan oil boom, as the worldwide market for oil experienced a dramatic decline in oil prices. He also lacked both cleverness and subtlety. Some report concern that he may have a paranoid personality. At the least, he seems to have a high-conflict personality with plenty of Targets of Blame.

> Maduro's lack of trust of those outside his inner circle and the continuous quest for common enemies (either against himself or the government's social, economic and political project) has been present in his discourse and sometimes displayed very vehemently in his social media strategy.[181]

As the following shows, he appears to be increasingly authoritarian.

Fantasy Crisis

Maduro's recipe for creating a crisis was as simple as it was brutal: blame all of Venezuela's problems on "counterrevolutionaries," and apply that term to anyone and everyone he wanted to defeat.

He also sees himself and his country as under attack from the United States.

> Socialist President Nicolas Maduro said Wednesday that he has uncovered an assassination plot that leads directly to the White House. Venezuela's leader repeated his frequent warning that a U.S. invasion is imminent—this time giving some details but no evidence. . . . President Donald Trump early in his administration publicly mused about using the "military option" to remove Maduro from power, with advisers urging against the idea.[182]

It's hard to know how much of this fear is fantasy and how much could be real. This is one of the problems in trying to understand a relationship between two potential HCPs.

Fantasy Villains

Maduro has gradually become more extreme: he jails his political opponents and is labeling more and more people as counterrevolutionaries.

> The revolution had so far been lenient, he said, but it was time that "counter-revolutionaries" be handled "with justice and firmness." He acknowledged that it was not easy for outsiders to understand what was going on in Venezuela. "This is a revolution," he said. "And we're in the midst of an acceleration of the revolutionary process."[183]

He sees the United States as a Target of Blame coordinating with his opponents. On December 9, 2018, a *New York Times* article states that "Maduro said many opposition leaders are waiting for a U.S.-led invasion without giving details."[184]

Fantasy Hero

Maduro has always seen himself as a revolutionary hero, with a drive for more and more power. In order to gain complete control, in 2017 he rewrote the constitution and replaced the legislature:

> The National Assembly, where the opposition holds a majority, has censured him for "abandoning the Presidency" and consistently foiled his initiatives. Maduro, frustrated, decided to simply create his own legislature—a replacement body, filled with loyalists, that was empowered to rewrite the country's constitution. Throughout the spring, his struggle with the opposition inspired a four-month confrontation between the government and protesters in which scores of people died and hundreds were injured. Finally, in July, Maduro successfully held elections for the new body, which he called the constituent assembly. The protests died out, and, for the first time since becoming President, he seemed firmly in control.[185]

But by the time of this writing in January 2019, Maduro's country is predictably in shambles; many of its people are impoverished, and some are on the verge of starvation. He gives special treatment to those who swear absolute loyalty, but millions of Venezuelans have fled to neighboring countries. Maduro's hold on power appears to be unraveling, with a strengthening opposition and weakening allies. But this can be the most dangerous time, when Wannabe Kings lash out and tighten their control.

High-Emotion Media

Maduro tries to make effective use of television in a similar way to Chavez; he has a folksy style just like his mentor, although not as appealing.

> Maduro's speeches are blunt and provocative, animated by a bumptious sense of humor and a voice that suggests someone who has spent a great deal of time rallying crowds without a microphone. As cameras rolled, he delivered an hour-long soliloquy—a mixture of folksy homilies, socialist slogans, jokes, and bluster, centered on his victory over his political opponents.[186]

Once again, television may be the most powerful form of high-emotion media that is made to order for this Wannabe King. But it may not be enough.

👑 👑 👑

Italy: Berlusconi and the Next Wannabe Kings

Italy was one of the European nations that went in big for democracy after the end of World War II. Before that war, in 1922, the king of Italy appointed Benito Mussolini as prime minister. He was the head of the Fascist Party, which was very nationalistic and believed in having a dictator. They declared a Fascist state in Italy in 1925, with Mussolini as the leader ("Il Duce"). He was popular and led the nation into an alliance with Germany's like-minded dictator Adolf Hitler.

However, by 1943, when World War II was going badly for Italy, Mussolini's Fascist Party turned on him. He was arrested and subsequently executed in 1945. His body was hung by its feet in the public square for all to see what had become of him. In 1946, Italy's monarchy ended and it became a democracy. It has remained a democracy ever since; however, the arrival of Silvio Berlusconi on the national political scene in the 1990s apparently put that in jeopardy—up to the present.[187]

Berlusconi's Early Years

Silvio Berlusconi was born in 1936 in Milan. His father was a bank clerk and his mother was a housewife. He and his family suffered through the carpet bombings of the Allied forces during World War II, with bombs landing as close as his own street. He reports that he was close to his mother and that after his father came home from the war, he "walked around with pure sunshine in his pocket."[188]

Berlusconi grew up in a tough lower-middle-class neighborhood with plenty of troublemakers around. At school he got bullied, until one day he fought back; after that, he was never bullied again and became a leader. He was known as a quick study at school and highly entrepreneurial. He made money helping other students study.[189]

At the age of twenty-five, he made his first real estate deal. He took that industry by storm and eventually became a billionaire. Then, when government rules made it easier to own a TV and media business, he took that industry by storm too.[190] Then he set his sights on politics.

High-Conflict Personality

Berlusconi was the prime minister of Italy for nine years (off and on, spanning the years between 1994 to 2011)—the-longest serving prime minister since WWII. He showed many signs of being an HCP Wannabe King during his two administrations. In 2012, after nearly twenty years in Italian politics, he was convicted of tax fraud and was facing expulsion from the Italian Senate. At that time, a psychologist said he had a personality disorder:

> As Silvio Berlusconi prepares to face a vote on his explusion [sic] from parliament on Wednesday evening, one of Italy's leading psychologists has said the former prime minister shows signs of "madness" and has a "personality disorder".
>
> The diagnosis was made by Luigi Cancrini during an interview with Radio 24.
>
> He said Berlusconi, who in July was convicted of tax fraud by the supreme court—his first definitive criminal conviction, has "narcissistic personality disorder."[191]

Fantasy Crisis

In the early 1990s, Italy faced many financial woes and *all five* of the country's left-leaning governing parties were the subjects of corruption investigations. Berlusconi came into office as an independent, brash, overbearing personality. He sold himself as the only viable savior of a struggling nation: he was the political outsider who would save Italy from the villainized, vanquished government that had lost power and was on the way out because of these investigations. He promised to restore the country to international prominence.[192]

Fantasy Villains

His villains were the five pro-western governing parties, including former communists and liberals. He claimed that these groups were stripping Italians of their privileges—and increasing their taxes.

Fantasy Hero

Berlusconi promised that, if elected, he would provide wealth and grandeur for all, as well as a million more jobs. He would solve their debt crisis with the European Union. These promises were obvious and transparent lies—and, of course, impossible to achieve.[193]

Berlusconi also launched a massive campaign of advertisements for himself on his three TV networks. "I am the Jesus Christ of politics," Berlusconi claimed in one ad.[194]

Berlusconi won the prime minister's job but delivered on none of his promises. Nevertheless, the narrative he told, over and over, was so effective that Italians repeatedly forgave his complete failure to make good on those promises—as well as for his own corruption.

In 2013, Berlusconi was convicted of tax fraud and given a four-year prison sentence. Because he was over 70 years old, he was exempted from direct imprisonment and instead served his sentence by doing unpaid community service. Berlusconi was also caught up in a variety of scandals involving many prostitutes, including one who was underage.[195]

High-Emotion Media

Not surprisingly, Berlusconi has had significant control of Italian media, especially television.

> For the past thirty years, Italian Prime Minister Silvio Berlusconi's family has controlled Italy's top three national TV channels, known as the Mediaset empire. As head of government, Berlusconi has also maintained a tight grip on the "public service" national broadcaster, Radiotelevisione Italiana (Rai). Together, Mediaset and Rai control roughly 90 percent of national audience and advertising revenue shares.
>
> . . .
>
> This has made broadcast media coverage increasingly partisan. Berlusconi and his government have repeatedly attempted to muzzle critical Italian media and avoid scrutiny. Now, the only significant criticism of the government comes from a handful of print outlets and a few isolated voices within Rai.
>
> Berlusconi allegedly complained about critical voices within Rai and put pressure on the directors to silence dissent. Past disclosures leaked to the media have implicated Berlusconi and his allies in various corruption affairs.[196]

Although Berlusconi couldn't run for office again because of his conviction for fraud, he was able to lead a party into the 2018 elections. Although his party actually came in third, his influence helped create an atmosphere of anger that led to the victories of two other antiestablishment parties.

As of this writing in 2019, the government of Italy is struggling to agree on leadership and policies. Apparently anger at the establishment, stoked by Berlusconi for years, does not seem to provide a reality-based set of policies or focus. Fantasy crises seem to have their limits when the reality of overturning the status quo starts to settle in.

It's also interesting to note Berlusconi's highly narcissistic and aggressive personality, which helped him become a real estate and media mogul, drove his multitude of false promises, his bitter attacks on other politicians, his control of the media, and his many grandiose statements about himself. Did he have sociopathic traits as well? His conviction for tax fraud and allegations of many other crimes suggest that he did. All of these characteristics appear to be similar to those of Donald Trump in the United States. Will the outcome be the same? Only time will tell.

Conclusion

All of these national leaders appear to be Wannabe Kings, using fantasy crises to gain power, while villainizing vulnerable groups of people specific to each one's country, and playing the image of a hero—a charming strongman who can talk for hours on television. In fact, they own, control, or influence much of the television media.

Will these HCPs succeed in the complete takeover of their governments and lead their countries into war against their fantasy villains? Only time will tell. But if they have narcissistic and sociopathic personalities, they are unlikely to stop in their quest for unlimited power. Others will have to stop them, if their voters can't or don't want to.

HERE AT HOME:
FROM MCCARTHY TO NIXON
TO TRUMP TO _____?

The United States has had several flirtations with HCP Wannabe Kings throughout the history of our democracy. In the past century, they have received a surprising amount of support from potential voters.

> Americans have long had an authoritarian streak. It was not unusual for figures such as Coughlin, Long, McCarthy, and Wallace to gain the support of a sizable minority—30 or even 40 percent—of the country.[197]

Father Charles Coughlin was an immensely popular anti-Semitic Catholic priest in the 1930s who was openly opposed to democracy and questioned the value of elections. His nationalist radio program reached 40 million listeners a week, and he packed stadiums and auditoriums with people who wanted to hear him speak.

Huey Long was a Depression Era governor and then a senator for Louisiana. He was known for being a demagogue with dictatorial tendencies. He used bribes and threats to get what he wanted from legislators, judges, and the press. He called for the redistribution of wealth and his movement, Share Our Wealth, had almost eight million names on its mailing list.

In 1968 and 1972, Alabama's governor George Wallace ran for president on a platform that opposed school integration and appealed to working-class whites' sense of being left out of the nation's economic progress. He made significant inroads into the Democratic Party until an assassination attempt halted his candidacy in 1972. At that time, he had a million more votes than George McGovern, who became the party's candidate and who subsequently lost in a landslide to Richard Nixon.[198]

Although it appears that all the Wannabe Kings in this chapter are on the political right, there have been HCPs on the left as well. Remember, it's not about the politics; it's about the personalities. A notable example was Jim Jones, a revolutionary preacher and leader of the People's Temple in the San Francisco Bay Area in the 1970s. He took 900 followers with him to Guyana in South America to create a socialist utopian community. Unfortunately, his paranoia got the best of him, along with his apparently narcissistic and sociopathic tendencies, and he led his followers into the largest mass murder-suicide in American history.[199]

Joseph McCarthy

The most widely known and popular authoritarian politician in America was Joseph McCarthy. He was a US senator from Wisconsin from 1947 to 1957.

McCarthy's Early Years

McCarthy grew up on a farm in Wisconsin. One of nine children, he was shy but "favored by a protective mother."[200] In his twenties, he became a lawyer and went into politics. Although originally a Democrat, he lost his bid to be a district attorney and changed his party to Republican and went on to become the youngest judge in the state. However, he apparently lied during the campaign and said his opponent was much older and that he was younger than he actually was. Apparently, his pattern of lying in politics was already established by his twenties. He was involved in at least one suspicious case as a judge, but he was eventually elected as a senator for Wisconsin.

High-Conflict Personality

McCarthy was at first a quiet and undistinguished senator. But apparently he had lied about his record during World War II and was also involved in a bit of tax fraud, so he decided he needed an issue "to distract attention from his affairs." In 1950, he settled on communism, to exploit American's fears of a Communist takeover. When World War II ended, Americans were concerned about the spread of Communism because Russia and China had become Communist. In 1950, North Korea invaded South Korea—only to be pushed back with the help of the United States. The Cold War was in full swing. He certainly fulfilled the Target of Blame aspect of a high-conflict personality as well as a possible sociopathic personality given the extent of his lying and willingness to destroy people's reputations for his own benefit.

Fantasy Crisis

Although people were somewhat worried about Communism, McCarthy amped up the threat dramatically, sparking an explosion of anti-Communist paranoia aimed at promoting his own influence. McCarthy claimed, without any evidence, that there were hundreds of Communists—every one of them disloyal to the United States—working undercover, especially in the federal government and in Hollywood.

Fantasy Villains

To anyone who would listen, he insisted that these spies needed to be rooted out—and that no one was doing enough in that regard. McCarthy stepped into the imaginary breach and took charge as America's self-appointed scourge of Communism. He accused innumerable people of disloyalty, hauled in thousands of ordinary citizens for questioning, and demanded that US government employees go to excessive lengths to prove their devotion to their country.

Thousands of people, especially in government and the film industry, lost their jobs because of McCarthy's efforts. Many were blacklisted from their fields for years or decades. McCarthy was extremely media savvy and used the new medium of television to boost his visibility in many American homes. He kept the country spellbound by holding televised hearings in the US Senate. In these hearings, McCarthy aggressively questioned people about their ties to Communism and their relationships with other people who might be Communists.

Fantasy Hero

Eventually McCarthy became the most powerful and visible person in Congress. Many elected officials feared him and what he could do to them. In 1950,

McCarthy claimed that he had a list of over 200 US State Department employees who were "known Communists." There was, of course, no such list. Nevertheless, the claim sparked nationwide hysteria. McCarthy refused to provide the names of any of these people and was unable to produce any coherent or reasonable evidence that Communists worked at the State Department.[201]

One of McCarthy's most high-profile supporters was Richard Nixon. As vice president during Dwight Eisenhower's first term as president, Nixon endorsed Senator Joe McCarthy's wild witch hunts. Nixon shifted his position only after McCarthy slandered Eisenhower and became a liability to the Republican Party.[202] Although McCarthy scared millions of Americans, he was able to consolidate enormous power and make his own name a household word. Nevertheless, during his entire anti-Communism campaign, McCarthy successfully fingered exactly zero Communists.

High-Conflict Media

Just as Hitler was the first politician to use the radio to connect intimately with ordinary people in their homes, McCarthy was the first politician to use television in a similar intensely emotional, repetitive manner. He dominated television news for four years. But his power collapsed in 1954 when he accused the US Army of coddling known Communists. He overreached.[203]

Televised hearings of his Army investigation let the American people see his bullying tactics and lack of credibility, and he quickly lost support. Eventually, McCarthy's own political party turned against him. In 1954, the Senate censured him for his aggressive tactics, and all but one senator voted against him. This vote "effectively end[ed] his career,"[204] but he still had popular support until his death from likely alcoholism in 1957.

> At the height of McCarthy's political power, polls showed that nearly half of all Americans approved of him. Even after the Senate's 1954 censure of him, McCarthy enjoyed 40 percent support in Gallup polls.[205]

It appears that his emotional repetition was in isolation because of the lack of any competing voice or television broadcasts. Television was new in the 1950s, so it had the authority of a single voice. Since McCarthy was a senator, he obviously was someone to be highly regarded, and no other television station was going to criticize him—especially regarding the hot topic of Communism.

This allowed him to gain a tremendous following by focusing so intensely on his fantasy villains. It was high-conflict drama from start to finish. For four years the country was captivated and many careers were ruined. When the nation finally caught on to the dangerousness of people like him, they called it *McCarthyism*. His aggressiveness and his lack of empathy and remorse in publicly and pointlessly humiliating people appears to fit well into the Wannabe King pattern. He is a classic example of promoting a Fantasy Crisis Triad using the latest potentially high-conflict medium—television.

♕ ♕ ♕

Richard Nixon

Richard Nixon was president of the United States from 1969 to 1974, when he resigned from office during his second term. He was faced with likely impeachment charges because of his role in the Watergate scandal involving a break-in to the Democratic Party's headquarters during the 1972 election.

Nixon's Early Years

Much has been written about Richard Nixon's difficult personality. He was named after King Richard the Lion-Hearted, and three of his four brothers were also named after kings (he was the second oldest). His mother was emotionally unavailable for a lot of his early childhood due to illness and caring for the other children, so he often stayed with relatives and apparently cried a lot. At the same time, he also showed a tendency toward self-reliance, a quiet seriousness, and a precocious maturity.

He was a quick study with a remarkable memory. He could read before he started school and read over thirty books on his own in first grade. He was known to enjoy reading rather than playing outside. His parents encouraged his intellectual specialness, although his father could also be very mean-spirited and physically abusive.[206]

High-Conflict Personality

Some authors say that his childhood of emotional deprivation and specialness led to him developing a narcissistic personality.

> We will now observe the manifestations of a narcissistic personality in Nixon, providing examples of how he repeatedly attempted to prove to himself and others his right to be "number one" and how he denied his dependency, rage, and envy. At times when the reality of his environment

or his own internal turmoil threatened his grandiosity he would feel humiliated, enraged, envious, physically ill, paranoid, and willing to strike back at "unloving" others or dangerous things in order to reaffirm his grandiosity.[207]

How much of his personality was inborn and how much was due to his early childhood is hard to know. Did his king-like name and upbringing make him want to be in charge and to dominate others? We will never know. But he appears to have had the makings of a brilliant politician who was brought down by his own highly aggressive personality.

Another important aspect of his self-defeating personality was his constant lying. In a psychologically informed biography, Fawn Brodie explained:

Nixon lied in matters both important and trivial. She stated that "Nixon lied to gain love, to store up his grandiose fantasies, to bolster his ever-wavering sense of identity. He lied in attacks, hoping to win. . . . And always he lied, and this most aggressively, to deny that he lied. . . . Finally, he enjoyed lying." She gives examples of Nixon's lying in matters large and small: He lied about his college major, about his wife's first name and birth date, about his own secret slush fund in the 1952 Presidential campaign, and in the Watergate cover-up.[208]

Fantasy Crisis

Nixon ran for president in 1968, after serving as a congressman and a US senator from California. At the time, Americans were deeply concerned about—and deeply divided on—two major issues: civil rights and the Vietnam War. During the 1960s, the US was being torn apart by protests, marches, and riots. After major civil rights laws were passed in 1964 and 1965, many state and local governments in the south refused to enforce them.

Meanwhile, in Vietnam, America was fighting a war for reasons that many people could not comprehend. Over 30,000 Americans had already died by 1968. Although the Vietnamese saw this as a civil war, many American politicians sold it to their countrymen as a fight against Communism.

As a law-and-order presidential candidate, Nixon was able to reassure Americans that he would push back against the forces of chaos and change what was happening in the country. For example, one essay he wrote in the lead-up to the election year was titled: "If Mob Rule Takes Hold in America—A Warning from Richard Nixon."[209]

Fantasy Villains

Nixon's law-and-order platform was a brilliant catch-all for numerous villains. Depending on what scared a particular person, "chaos" could be a reference to protestors, especially students; to civil rights activists and advocates; to non-white people in general; or to Communists. (Recall Nixon's earlier support of McCarthy.)

Fantasy Hero

Nixon's implied stance against civil rights also enabled him to win the votes of many southerners, who felt betrayed by the prior president's (Lyndon Johnson's) "concessions" to racial equality with the Civil Rights Act of 1964 and Voting Rights Act of 1965. Also, there had been riots in the inner cities in the 1960s and the war in Vietnam was gaining protesters. In 1968, Nixon ran as a Republican antiwar candidate, stealing the Democrats issue. He showed ads with war footage and "Nixon's calm voice promising to end the war and correct the mistakes of the old set of leaders who were responsible."[210] Of course, Nixon didn't end the Vietnam war, he even expanded it secretly into Cambodia.[211]

But Nixon won the presidency in 1968 and again in 1972. As president, Nixon proved lawless and paranoid. He illegally wiretapped and spied on his perceived enemies and hired a group of thugs to break into Democratic National Headquarters in the Watergate complex in Washington.

In 1973, when federal investigators began looking into his crimes, he fired independent special prosecutor Archibald Cox. Nine months later, the US House of Representatives filed articles of impeachment against Nixon who resigned from office less than two weeks afterward.

High-Emotion Media

Nixon had an adversarial relationship with the news media before he even ran for the office of president. He blamed the media for his loss to John F. Kennedy in his run for president in 1960.

However, in January 1968, before his comeback presidential election campaign got going, he met Roger Ailes when he appeared on *The Mike Douglas Show*, a television variety show, which was watched by seven million housewives. Ailes was the show's producer and Nixon soon hired Ailes to teach him how to appear warmer and more human on screen. But that was not enough for Nixon. His battle with the media continued.

> Nixon, like Lyndon Johnson before him, realized the political value of prime-time speeches carried free by the networks. Faced with an increasing number of presidential addresses, the networks started to seek balance to this powerful White House platform by following them with commentary. So while the networks carried the speech, to Nixon's great chagrin, they followed it with analysis and criticism.
>
> Nixon would not stand for this. Within two weeks, the administration dispatched Vice President Spiro Agnew to deliver a withering assault on the networks in front of a Republican audience in Des Moines. The networks dutifully carried the speech live after the White House instructed them that it was in their best interest to do so.[212]

Nixon went on to look into ways that he could attack the networks by using the Federal Communications Commission, the Internal Revenue Service, and the Department of Justice. He did succeed in winning some concessions from them, for instance, CBS agreed to drop its immediate analysis after presidential and vice-presidential speeches.[213]

Nixon used the media to get his emotionally repetitive message out about law and order. But he also tried to get his message out in isolation, by blocking any responses to his speeches (and those of his vice president) by the media.

☙ ☙ ☙

Donald Trump

At the time of this writing (January 2019), Donald J. Trump is president of the United States. It's unknown how long he will stay in office as there are many investigations going on about his possible election collusion with the Russian government in 2016 and other possibly fraudulent financial matters. Yet his political base sticks with him, he has a Republican majority in the Senate, and the Supreme Court is majority conservative, including two of his own appointees. And he has already filed for his re-election bid in 2020.

Regardless of the outcome of these investigations, his election stirred up a heated national debate over whether he is dangerous or good for America; whether he is a pathological liar or authentic; and whether democracy has been harmed or strengthened by his presidency.

Trump's Early Years

Donald Trump was born into a wealthy real estate family in New York City. Apparently, he was brash and difficult to manage, even from an early age. He was known as a bully who wanted to overpower people. If he made a false statement, he would simply defend it and repeat it several times to make others believe it was true.

> In elementary school, Donny impressed classmates with his athleticism, shenanigans and refusal to acknowledge mistakes, even one so trivial as misidentifying a popular professional wrestler. . . .
>
> "When I look at myself in the first grade and I look at myself now, I'm basically the same," the 70-year-old presumptive Republican nominee once told a biographer. "The temperament is not that different."[214]
>
> Trump's father taught him that there were winners and losers in life, and that Trumps had to be winners. "Be a killer," his father told his sons, as if training them to develop narcissistic traits.[215]

High-Conflict Personality

Trump appears to have numerous Targets of Blame, a lot of all-or-nothing thinking and solutions, frequent unmanaged emotions and extreme behavior, and threats of extreme behavior.

When the younger Trump became a Manhattan real estate developer, he was extremely demanding and inconsistent with his employees. He blamed them for his own decisions.

> "Who said to make this ceiling so low?"
>
> "You knew about this, Donald," Hyde replied. "We talked about it, if you remember, and the plans—"
>
> Abruptly Donald leaped up and punched his fist through the tile. Then he turned on Hyde in a rage. . . . The tirade went on at great length as Trump "humiliated [Hyde] in front of twenty people, colleagues and professionals."[216]

Over the course of the first two years of his presidency, it was common for me to hear people of both political parties discussing his narcissistic traits. Little was said about sociopathic traits; however, this too started becoming a topic of discussion after several of his cohorts were convicted of crimes committed while working for him. Does he have a personality disorder? I won't answer that question because it is a mental health diagnosis. You will have to decide for yourself.

Fantasy Crisis

There are so many examples of Trump's use of Fantasy Crisis Triads to gain power that I will only focus on one in detail here, Mexican immigrants. I will mention several others briefly, but how he has handled the immigration issue is a good example of how he has promoted and handled all the rest.

In 2010, after years of donating to both Democratic and Republican political candidates (80 percent to Democrats at that time), he spoke with consultants and consciously decided to run for President as a conservative Republican.[217]

In 2011, perhaps as a campaign warm-up, he widely promoted the extreme view of some Republicans that President Barack Obama (an African-American elected president in 2008) was born in Africa and therefore not allowed to be president. This apparently resonated with a majority of Republicans. In 2016, he admitted that Obama was born in the US (in Hawaii), but he was so successful with his repetition of this fantasy crisis about Obama that even a year later 51 percent of Republicans still believed Obama was born in Africa.[218]

Trump then focused on Mexican immigration:

> In preparation for his presidential bid, he instructed his aides to listen to thousands of hours of conservative talk radio. They reported back to Trump that "the GOP base was frothing over a handful of issues," one of which was immigration.[219]

For this crisis, Trump claimed that Mexicans were illegally pouring across the southern United States border, hurting unemployed citizens' job prospects and creating terrible danger for US citizens. He didn't mention that the number of Mexicans coming north into the United States was the lowest it had been since 2009.

> There are more Mexicans leaving the United States than coming in. According to the Pew Research Center, there was a net outflow of 140,000 from 2009 to 2014. If Trump builds his wall, he'll lock more Mexican immigrants in than he'll keep out. . . .
>
> One study of 103 cities between 1994 and 2004 found that violent crime rates decreased as the concentration of immigrants increased. Numerous studies have shown that a big share of the drop in crime rates in the 1990s is a result of the surge in immigration.[220]

Fantasy Villains

Despite these facts, Trump went ahead and made Mexican immigrants into his fantasy villains. In his very first speech when he announced his candidacy, he said this:

> When Mexico sends its people, they're not sending their best. They're not sending you. They're not sending you. They're sending people that have lots of problems, and they're bringing those problems with us. They're bringing drugs. They're bringing crime. They're rapists. And some, I assume, are good people.[221]

Fantasy Hero

In the same speech, he went on to say that he would be the incredible hero, saving America and making it great again.

> I will be the greatest jobs president that God ever created. I tell you that. I'll bring back our jobs from China, from Mexico, from Japan, from so many places. I'll bring back our jobs, and I'll bring back our money.[222]

And of course, at his presidential inauguration he famously said: "I alone can fix it."[223] The fantasy hero.

Looking back on his "Mexican rapists" announcement speech, we realize that it's very similar to the speeches he has continued to make throughout his time in office. He is brilliant at using emotional repetition, even repeating his own phrases on a regular basis.

And his solution to the fantasy crisis of Mexicans pouring in?

> I would build a great wall, and nobody builds walls better than me, believe me, and I'll build them very inexpensively, I will build a great, great wall on our southern border. And I will have Mexico pay for that wall.[224]

Of course, this too was a fantasy and Mexico was never going to pay for it. By January 2019, almost two years into his presidency, his overwhelmingly Republican congress had still refused to provide the funding for his great wall. Putting up this wall would be humiliating for Mexico, but making them pay for it would be doubly so, and totally unrealistic.

This statement fits with a personality that is into dominating and humiliating others without empathy or remorse, with a bit of paranoia and a touch of sadism thrown in. These are the characteristics of a malignant narcissist. Could his first speech indicate that Trump is one? He certainly has Targets of Blame. From the first day of his presidential campaign, the signs of an extreme Wannabe King were already there for those who knew what to look for.

More Fantasy Crises

Trump has had many other fantasy crises. He put a lot of energy into trying to eliminate Obamacare, also known as the Affordable Care Act, the healthcare expansion that was promoted by his predecessor, President Barack Obama. But a funny thing happened on the way to Obamacare (ACA) repeal. After the election, polls showed that the majority of Americans actually supported the ACA and didn't want it repealed.[225]

The Republican Congress did not fall in line with the new president on this issue after all, and Trump's efforts to end it failed when the Senate gave the repeal thumbs down six months into his presidency in July 2017.

> Since Trump became president, his promise to repeal and replace the Affordable Care Act is nowhere close to being fulfilled, despite his repeated, confident assertions on the campaign trail that it could be done in just a day. The failure of health-care legislation in the Senate this week shows Trump still has not learned how to navigate Congress—and how much he is struggling to be the dealmaker, fighter and winner he portrayed himself to be to voters.[226]

Another fantasy crisis for Trump was his claim that scientific reports on climate change were a liberal plot against business and he did not believe in it. So early in his administration he cancelled the participation of the United States in the Paris Climate Accord, which had been painstakingly negotiated among many countries.[227]

He decided that trade wars were "easy to win" and attacked Canada and European allies, along with China. Although some politicians and economists agree that the United States needed to address trade issues with China, Trump's eager pursuit of wide-ranging trade wars was his idea and his alone—another demonstration of his all-or-nothing thinking. He even lost his own appointed chief economic adviser, Gary Cohn, over it.[228]

With Canada, he said there was a terrible trade deficit, but he only mentioned goods. When services were taken into account, the US actually had a positive balance in trade with Canada. Even though this was the case, Trump forced the renegotiation of the North American Free Trade Agreement (NAFTA) with Mexico and Canada. Although only minor changes were made (to the relief of most politicians and economists), Trump claimed a huge victory.[229]

This surprised almost no one, as his grandiose claims are growing quite familiar to most Americans. After the Democrats won back control of the House of Representatives in the November 2018 congressional elections, indications are that Trump is starting to lose his grip, even with his base of white working-class men. "[I]t is no surprise that more than half of white working class men now believe that Mr. Trump is 'self-dealing' and corrupt."[230] Reality is beginning to set in.

US Presidential Election 2016

Donald Trump decided to base his campaign on Mexican immigrants, Muslims, journalists, China, and many other fantasy crises. Figure 5 is a summary of how his Fantasy Crisis Triads worked in emotionally splitting the voters four ways, resulting in his election win in 2016. Although his percentage of votes was slightly less than his opponent, Hillary Clinton, he won in the Electoral College, which gives states with smaller populations an advantage over more populous states.

Trump won nearly 63 million votes, which is 28 percent of the total possible votes. Hillary Clinton won nearly 66 million votes, which is 29 percent. Third parties won nearly 8 million votes, which is 4 percent.[231] This leaves 39 percent of eligible adults who didn't vote at all in the 2016 election.[232]

Most of the voter information I use here comes from a detailed analysis by three political science researchers published late in 2018 in a book titled *Identity Crisis: The 2016 Presidential Campaign and the Battle for the Meaning of America.* The 4-Way Voter Split group analysis is my own.

LOYALISTS

Trump's support included Republicans who shared his negative views of his various Targets of Blame. For example, according to polls, "68 percent of Republican primary voters believed that Trump's statements about Mexican immigrants being rapists who bring drugs and crime into the country was 'basically right.'"[233] But approximately one-third of Republicans did not agree with those statements and didn't vote for him in the primary election. "Among Republicans who did not support Trump in the primary, nearly seven in ten (69%) voted for him in the general election." They stayed loyal to the Republican Party candidate.

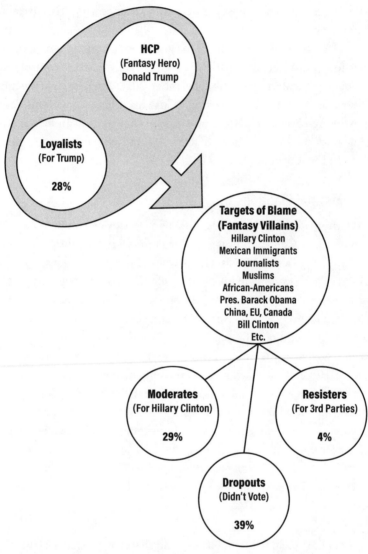

FIGURE 5. US presidential election 2016—4-way voter split. *Copyright © 2019 Bill Eddy, All Rights Reserved,* Why We Elect Narcissists and Sociopaths—And How We Can Stop, *Berrrett-Koehler Publishers*

MODERATES

Moderates are the emotionally mild group of voters, which includes many Republican moderates, Democratic moderates, and most Independents. This is typically the largest group of voters and it decides most elections.

Moderates generally are not the energized party bases. In many ways they are comfortable with the "establishment" and don't like a lot of intense political conflict. In this election, Moderates went in four directions, some into each of the four split groups.

In my analysis the Moderate candidate in this fundamentally two-party system was Hillary Clinton in 2016. The majority of the country voted for her by almost 3 million votes more than Trump. They remained Moderate.

Double Negatives

Double Negatives is the term given by the *Identity Crisis* researchers to those voters who had equally unfavorable views of both Clinton and Trump. I believe that this is because of the effect of Trump's intense emotional splitting or dividing of groups as he attacked Clinton and other targets in almost every one of his public announcements or Twitter commentaries.

The effect of emotional splitting is that it triggers an equally distasteful feeling about both people, even though one (the HCP) is usually acting extremely badly while the other (the Target of Blame) is being fairly normal or simply defending himself or herself. The result of repeatedly hearing very bad things about a normal person from a very badly behaving HCP is that both are perceived as equally very bad. I've seen this over and over again, in high-conflict divorcing families, workplace conflicts, and legal disputes. People turn away from *both* the HCP and their Target of Blame.

By consistently attacking Clinton about having a private email server when she was Secretary of State (a potentially illegal set-up because of the risk of releasing government secrets, but this didn't happen, and she was cleared), Trump was able to make her seem involved in a scandal and dishonest. This turned out to be a fantasy crisis. Ironically, she was unable to pin any one scandal on him, because there were so many and she didn't effectively focus on one the way he did.

> In an early October YouGov poll, almost 80 percent of respondents said that they had "heard a lot" about the Clinton email story—more than any other story about Clinton or Trump. (For example, only 51% said they had heard a lot about Trump's calling Alicia Machado "Miss Piggy.") . . . Meanwhile, no single idea or theme dominated perceptions of Trump.[234]

In this election, more double-negative voters were Republican: 45 percent to 35 percent Democrat. "Trump did better among those with unfavorable views of both candidates. They appeared to be holding their nose and voting their partisanship."[235] Those double-negative Moderate Republicans voted with the Loyalists. Most of the double-negative Moderate Democrats stayed put and voted for Clinton. But some voted against both and went with the Resisters by voting for third-party candidates, and some went with the Dropouts and did not vote at all.

Independent Voters

Independent voters are a growing part of the electorate and generally are Moderates. However, 75 percent of these voters lean toward one party or the other, while the remaining 25 percent are likely to drop out and not vote at all.[236] If they mostly vote with their parties, then why do they register as Independents? Surveys and interviews have shown that they basically "don't like political parties," "are tired of the fighting between both the Republican and Democratic political parties," and " . . . think that there is a need for balance and compromise, and so . . . [they are] independent[s]."[237]

In my view, they essentially don't like the fighting and therefore fit my category of emotionally-mild Moderates. In 2016, 68 percent of Independents who lean Republican voted for Trump, and 65 percent of Independents who lean Democratic voted for Clinton. But as pollsters have noticed, "The characteristic anger and vitriol of partisan politics are turning them away from party membership. . . . In the wake of the 2016 election, we see mounting evidence of this connection between political dissatisfaction and independent identification."[238]

RESISTERS

Resisters can be the riled-up opponents of an HCP politician and they can be on the left or on the right, and sometimes both. But they also often attack the Moderates, which helps allow the HCP to be elected. In the case of Hitler, they were the Communists who often fought against the Social Democrats (the Moderate establishment), which weakened the Social Democrats and helped them lose power. In the case of Stalin's drive for collectivization in the Soviet Union, they were the small capitalist farmers who hid grain and equipment and mostly operated in the shadows. In Putin's Russia, they were the street protesters and others opposed to his policies. Every HCP inspires a resistance because of their extreme positions and extreme emotions.

In the 2016 election, Bernie Sanders represented the Resisters fighting against the Democratic establishment by running in the Democratic primaries against Hillary Clinton. However, he insisted that he remained an Independent. "Throughout the campaign, Sanders touted his independence, vowed to take on the political establishment, and railed against the Democratic National Committee."[239]

Clinton criticized Sanders for focusing on a few issues (free higher education, healthcare for all, and attacking big banks) with simplistic answers, while she had position papers and knowledge on just about every possible issue that could be raised.

On the other hand, Sanders' criticisms of Clinton and the Democratic Party were emotionally engaging to many of his followers. She became a Target of Blame for Sanders in an emotional way that mirrored Trump's attacks on her, although during most of the campaign Sanders and Clinton remained friendly.

However, late in the primaries, the release of emails hacked from the Democratic Party office revealed behind-the-scenes manipulations that added to the Resisters' anger at the establishment. As the primary campaign intensified, Sanders' followers' once generally favorable opinions of Clinton deteriorated significantly.

By the general election, after Sanders swung his support to Clinton, only 79 percent of his supporters voted for her, an estimated 12 percent voted for Trump, and the remainder continued resisting and voted for small third parties, or dropped out and didn't vote at all.[240]

With Sanders' more emotional relationship with his followers and his focus on simple, us-against-them anti-establishment messages, one wonders whether he might have been able to actually win the general election if he had been the Democratic candidate rather than Clinton. Sanders seemed to demonstrate the importance of an emotional bond with his followers, but without the emotional hostility toward Targets of Blame that Trump displayed.

DROPOUTS

In this election, the largest group of potential voters were the Dropouts at 39 percent. Dropouts have many reasons (or excuses) for not voting. I have often heard from those who believe there's no real difference between the parties or the candidates, or they are really busy, or they can't really get away from work on election day (even when they're self-employed).

One of the more recent reasons may be new "voter suppression" laws in several states that limit hours and locations and require limited forms of identification for voting. However, although such laws appear targeted at minority populations, such as African-Americans and Native Americans, these new laws do not appear to have changed the historical trend away from voting.

> However, African-Americans did vote less in 2016 for the first time in twenty years, even in states that had no changes in voter laws. Millennials and Generation X (18- to 35-year-olds) turned out more voters in 2016 than 2012, but still slightly less than 50 percent. [241]

A Fantasy Crisis Triad Overreach?

To help his party win the midterm congressional election in November 2018, Trump aggressively pursued the idea that a caravan of barefoot refugees from Central America was an "invasion of our country." He made the unfounded claim that it included "Middle Easterners" who were likely terrorists. So he ordered the Army to defend the border.[242]

> More than 5,000 active-duty military troops will deploy to the southern border by the end of this week, Defense Department officials said on Monday. . . . But the caravan, which has shrunk from 7,000 people to less than 3,500, is still weeks away from reaching the United States. [243]

It is not insignificant that immediately after the election, Trump stopped talking about this threat.

> "Now that the political utility of troops on the southern border to face a fictitious caravan invasion threat is over," said Adm. James G. Stavridis, a former commander of the military's Southern Command, "let's hope the president will stand down the troops so they can be with their families— especially over the holidays."[244]

It seemed that this fantasy crisis became obvious to a significant portion of the country, with the "fictitious caravan invasion" being openly discussed in major media outlets. In addition, the issue of immigration appears to be shifting all together in the eyes of the public, as revealed in November 2018.

> On Election Day, a stunning 54 percent of those who voted said immigrants "strengthen our country." Mr. Trump's party lost the national popular vote by seven points, but he lost the debate over whether immigrants are a strength or a burden by 20 points. Mr. Trump got more than half of Republicans to believe immigrants were a burden, but three quarters of Democrats and a large majority of independents concluded that America gains from immigration.[245]

When reality sets in enough, an HCP's fantasy crises seem to lose their power. But of course, with the use of high-emotion media, they often can keep covering up reality with more Fantasy Crisis Triads.

High-Emotion Media

When Trump campaigned for office, his way of speaking was far more emotional than all the other candidates, Democrat or Republican. This caught the attention of the Director of Content at dictionary.com, who said this about the words the presidential candidates were using during 2016:

> "Bernie [Sanders] and Hillary [Clinton] tend to use concrete language," she explained, "whereas the Republican contenders—with the possible exception of Kasich—tend to use descriptive language. I think that's partly why Trump's speech is so resonant with his supporters: he's speaking to them on an emotional plane."[246]

This fits very well with the theory of this book—that potentially high-conflict politicians use language that goes under everyone's radar and emotionally triggers them. Logically, none of these fantasy crises make any sense. But they make sense to narcissists, sociopaths, and high-conflict personalities who want to identify as many people as possible as villains so that voters view them as heroes by comparison. All of this works only on the emotional plane.

Trump also used emotional repetition in the names he chose to call people. He openly laughed and said he was adding a name to each of his opponents, just as Newt Gingrich taught Republican congressional candidates in the 1990s (see Chapter 4).

What he didn't say openly (and may or may not have even realized himself) was that he was tagging them with an emotional label. Our brains can't resist absorbing such labels, even without conscious processing. This is an extremely simple and emotional way to promote sales that advertisers learned decades ago but that most politicians are unwilling to use.

Also, these emotions triggered each voting group's own type of emotional responses; for instance, Loyalists might have felt joy, Resisters anger, Moderates fear and frustration, and Dropouts helplessness and/or avoidance. This further created division among all of these groups. "How can they (Loyalists, Resisters, Moderates, Dropouts) be so (stupid, overreactive, powerless, indifferent)?"

Furthermore, this emotional repetition was in isolation for many of Trump's followers who only got their news from Trump-favorable sources, such as Fox News. One analysis of Trump's electoral success clearly concluded that those who got their news from television and not from newspaper subscriptions were more susceptible to his emotional, but false, messages.

> The findings cover more than 1,000 mainstream news publications in more than 2,900 counties out of 3,100 nationwide from every state except Alaska, which does not hold elections at the county level.
>
> The results show a clear correlation between low subscription rates and Trump's success in the 2016 election, both against Hillary Clinton and when compared to Romney in 2012. Those links were statistically significant even when accounting for other factors that likely influenced voter choices, such as college education and employment, suggesting that the decline of local media sources by itself may have played a role in the election results. POLITICO's analysis suggests that Trump did, indeed, do worse overall in places where independent media could check his claims.[247]

Trump also directly attacked the media from the start of his campaign and trained his followers to do so too. At his rallies, he placed the media in a compact area where he could point at reporters and have the crowd jeer them. In this manner, he was able to cast doubt on their reporting, and he quickly adopted the phrase "fake news" when others reported accurately about him.

Rather than attempt to put news media out of business, as we have seen that other Wannabe Kings have done in other countries, Trump found great success in constantly criticizing them. Social media was also an important key to his success, but it was not necessarily the biggest factor. By using Twitter, Trump was able to communicate directly with his followers, but having his tweets *emotionally repeated* on cable and network television was far more important.

> It's also clear—as the economists Levi Boxell, Matthew Gentzkow and Jesse Shapiro wrote in these pages last year—that among older white Americans, the core demographic where first the primaries and then the general election were decided, television still far outstrips the internet as the most important source of news. And indeed, the three economists noted, for all the talk about Breitbart's influence and Russian meddling and dark web advertising, Trump only improved on Mitt Romney's showing among Americans who don't use the internet, and he "actually lost support among internet-using voters." In a sense, you could argue, all those tweets mattered mainly because they kept being quoted on TV.[248]

To put the power of the high-emotion media into perspective, the election researchers just mentioned reached three conclusions that really stood out to me:

1. The 2016 election was *not* really about economic anger or change. People were doing economically better than during the prior eight years when they elected an African-American president two times. The state of the economy helped Clinton win a majority of the national vote.

2. It really *was* about personality—the personality of the candidate and whether he or she wanted to unify or divide the nation. A nation can go either way. Barack Obama didn't make an issue of race, so people didn't vote based on that. Donald Trump did make an issue of race, so it "activated" people's residual racism more than their residual tolerance, and it helped him more.[249]

> What gave us the 2016 election, then, was not changes among voters. It was changes in the candidates…. [w]hat the candidates chose to do and say.[250]

And Wannabe Kings will do and say anything because they lack empathy or a conscience. Trump frequently said things such as "illegal immigrants are treated better in America than many of our vets,"[251] which isn't true but created a feeling of crisis—a fantasy crisis.

3. And it really *was* about the media repetition of emotional messages. "The news media value things that make for 'good stories'—interesting characters, novelty, drama, conflict, and controversy—and Trump supplied those in spades."[252] He received the most coverage.

♛ ♛ ♛

Conclusion: Who's Next?

Joe McCarthy had a history of lying in politics that began by the time he was in his twenties. He certainly had Targets of Blame and showed no empathy or remorse in falsely accusing them in public on television. He eventually had his downfall, but he still had a lot of support. *McCarthyism* is named after him.

Richard Nixon also lied a lot. He promoted an illegal scheme to break into the office of the Democratic Party headquarters at the Watergate Hotel during the election of 1972. He also had an enemies list, which was written down for him by his staff.

Donald Trump has been a good example of an HCP using Fantasy Crisis Triads to divide voters and win. This appears to be because today's high-emotion media, in all its forms, emphasizes faces, voices, and emotional messages. This ultimately favors high-conflict politicians (and all high-conflict personalities) who have far less self-restraint and ability to solve problems in the gray areas of real life.

Yet it seems that elections are no longer about good government, but about "good stories." In the all-or-nothing world of heroes and villains, Trump won.

But who will be next? Will it be someone on the far right or the far left? In Russia, the far-left Stalin was replaced (with a period of democracy in between) by a far-right Putin. In Hungary, pro-democracy Orban became far-right Orban.

Today's high-emotion media in America has helped create an environment in which a high-conflict personality can succeed with fantasy crises when real daily life is actually going okay for most people, including his followers. Yes, there are problems to be solved, but they don't compare to the problems that a Wannabe King can create in their endless quest for unlimited power.

10 COMMON MISTAKES WITH HIGH-CONFLICT POLITICIANS

In the examples in the prior chapters in this book, a minority of enthusiastic citizens made the mistake—or are currently making the mistake—of following Wannabe Kings to their own doom as well as everyone else's. In most cases, this minority was only 30 to 40 percent of the adult population. The other 60 to 70 percent of the potential electorate either opposed or came to oppose these HCP Wannabe Kings, but they too made many mistakes that no one should make in the future.

Mostly, they either believed and followed the Wannabe King, or allowed themselves to be split into at least three other groups, which allowed these Wannabe Kings to take power, and then gain more power, until they became unstoppable. As we have seen, after HCPs are elected and dismantle their democracies to impose authoritarian rule, it takes outside forces to stop them. We can no longer afford to let that happen anywhere in the world, so we must learn from the common mistakes so many have made.

Mistake 1: Missing the Warning Signs

In every case in this book, voters missed how dangerous and deceptive these HCP Wannabe Kings were until it was too late or almost too late. Some never varied from supporting their narcissistic and/or sociopathic leaders. In some cases, voters paid with their lives for not realizing that their endlessly aggressive HCP would turn on them eventually. You might wonder whether these voters and leaders saw any warning signs and had any doubts about the HCP early on when they could have voted against them.

The reality is that most didn't. They saw individual behaviors in isolation (a serious insult, a physical assault against someone else, a cruel joke, and so on) and didn't recognize that these individual behaviors were warning signs of patterns of future behavior. When you hitch your wagon to someone as grandiose, cruel, and lacking in empathy and remorse as these Wannabe Kings, you're going to get worse behavior in the future, not better. These voters naively believed the opposite.

Hitler, Stalin, and Mao routinely killed their closest colleagues to remove any perceived threats. Putin, Orban, Trump, and others appear to fire their closest colleagues on a regular basis to remove perceived threats or simply to show everyone who's boss. If everyone knew that high-conflict politicians are always adversarial and endlessly aggressive toward everyone (as you now know), then they would realize what was coming and that their loyalty means nothing to a Wannabe King even though the Wannabe King demands it all along.

I am hoping that this book will provide this general awareness and specific knowledge. It's important to know that this is an area of knowledge that you may not have needed in the past when there were fewer of these personalities present and they had less ability to impact your life. Now everyone needs to know these personality patterns and the warning signs.

Mistake 2: Believing in Fantasy Crises

Most of the high-conflict politicians described in this part of the book spent very little time explaining why their "crisis" was real and needed emergency action. They just presented it emotionally and quickly moved on to talk about their alleged villains and how they, the HCPs, were the "heroes." The crises became a given, an assumption.

In Germany, Loyalists just accepted that their loss of World War I, the reparations they had to pay to France, and the shambles of their economy were crises that could be blamed on a small group (1 percent) of people: Jews. Stalin and the Soviet government created famines in Russia and Ukraine, and then blamed them on the uncooperative peasants, the successful small farmers—the kulaks—who had worked hard doing what they thought was right. Mao created a devastating famine as well and destroyed the administrative and professional classes in an effort to protect the country from his own fantasy crises.

Orban and Trump have their immigrant "crises." Putin has his propaganda of homosexuals "crisis." Maduro's "crisis" was the counter-revolutionaries who were elected to the legislature among others.

Nowadays, this is where other politicians and the media make some of their biggest mistakes. They don't explain to the public *why* the supposed crisis is or is not a crisis—and that it might not even be a problem that needs solving. Instead, they uniformly focus on emotions—how people *feel* about the crisis, the villains, and the heroes. Journalists often interview alleged villains, alleged heroes, and everyday people and then ask how they feel.

And how does that make you feel? they ask. *And how do you feel about what so-and-so said about you-know-who today? And how do you feel about this politician? Would you still vote for him today? Thank you.* No useful information is provided in these types of conversations.

It's all about high emotions and high-conflict behavior that grab your attention. It's rarely about thoroughly examining the facts and honestly reporting that many of these alleged crises are actually nonexistent—or are problems that are already being or can be well-managed or solved.

Mistake 3: Believing in Fantasy Villains

Many people come to believe that the alleged villains really are villains. In the 1930s in the Soviet Union, the urban-based young revolutionaries went to the rural peasants in Ukraine to convince them to give up their small plots of land and join collectivized farms. They were convinced that these farmers were counterrevolutionaries and the cause of people being at risk of starving in the cities, when it was actually the Soviet government's policies that were causing food shortages.

A more recent example of this is the highly negative views of Hillary Clinton that were evoked by Donald Trump during the 2016 presidential election campaign. Trump said she was the most corrupt politician that had ever run for president, and he lead his followers in chants (even at the national Republican Party convention) to "Lock her up!" over her emails. Through this emotional repetition of such strong language, he gradually persuaded many people, even people who had decided that they would never vote for Trump, that Clinton was equally awful, so they would never vote for her either.

It is also amazing to see how successfully Vladimir Putin ran against his American villains (Hillary Clinton, George Soros, and US Ambassador McFaul) in his successful 2012 election bid for a third term as president.

Mistake 4: Believing in the Fantasy Hero

It was and is tempting to want a strongman form of leadership during a crisis. Narcissists and sociopaths know this, so they start their rise to power by persuading the nation there's a crisis that requires them to be the hero. If a population believes in this fantasy crisis, then they are much more likely to look for and accept a high-conflict politician as a good choice for leader. This is the message that Wannabe Kings have promoted through the ages—*I alone can fix this.* Many people believe that this is true—*We need a strong-man like this*—and that this is the person who should fulfill that role. But instead, they should recognize this statement as a warning sign.

Appearing strong helps Wannabe Kings gain and keep support from their followers. This appearance seems to be more important than actually doing things well. The following was written in May 2018, sixteen months into Trump's presidency and five months after he got a tax cut bill through congress:

> **Why Trump's approval has gone up, even as his scandals have piled up:**
> The vast majority of the American public long ago concluded that Donald Trump is a liar who does not "share their values" or "care about people like them." But at the start of his presidency, 79 percent of conservative Republicans believed that he could "get things done"—by December 2017, that had fallen to just 60 percent. Once the tax cuts passed, however, conservatives' confidence in Trump's "git 'er done" abilities spiked back up into the mid-70s.[253]

Wannabe Kings know that, above all else, they need to appear strong. And, as con artists, they are particularly skilled at making themselves into what their followers are looking for.

Mistake 5: Believing the HCP Has Been Victimized and Needs to Be Defended

From day one, Wannabe Kings present themselves to their followers as being victimized by their "villains." They ask for their followers' assistance in attacking these fantasy villains. This is a standard tactic of most narcissists and sociopaths, even those who have no interest in politics or leadership. It appears to be a natural trait for them: the HCPs get sympathy from others and then use it to get assistance in attacking the HCPs' Targets of Blame. This tactic works most of the time on the unwary. This is why understanding the traits of narcissists and sociopaths is such necessary knowledge for everyone in our modern times.

In Turkey, President Erdoğan appears to have traits of an HCP Wannabe King. He has repeatedly emphasized that the European Union is treating him unfairly and therefore, by extension, treating the citizens of Turkey unfairly, since the EU is reluctant to accept Turkey as a new member. In 2018, President Trump tried to isolate Erdoğan by imposing economic sanctions and public rebukes in an effort to quickly free a Christian minister who was being detained there. This tactic ended up helping Erdoğan:

> As the Turkish currency swoons, Erdogan has focused domestic anger instead against the United States and portrayed his country as the victim of intentional sabotage—shifting attention from economic problems that analysts said his government has failed for years to adequately address.[254]

So far, being attacked by Trump appears to have brought Erdoğan sympathy, not only with his own country's citizens, but with other leaders. But as the reality of economic problems increases, at some point his followers may realize that he is a fantasy hero and not a victim—and not the wonderful leader they thought he was.

Mistake 6: Believing the HCP Can Be Controlled

This common mistake is made with all narcissists and sociopaths. In the case of Adolf Hitler, many of those in business and government saw him as relatively harmless and controllable.

> There were those who met Hitler [in the 1920s] and recognized he represented almost a primeval force and possessed an uncanny ability to tap

into the emotions and anger of the German people, and those who dismissed him as a clownish figure who would vanish from the political scene as quickly as he had appeared.[255]

One banker with a history of working with the democratic government in the 1920s, Hjalmar Schacht, told an American reporter, Edgar Mowrer, that he was going to be meeting with Hitler in 1932:

> Three weeks later, Mower met Schacht again, and asked him how his conversation went with the Nazi leader. "Brilliantly," the German banker replied. "I've got that man right in my pocket."[256]

How wrong they were.

Likewise, when Donald Trump became president, many who elected him said that he would act "more presidential" once he got into office. He even made fun of this idea at rallies after being elected by pretending to be a serious and staid politician and then asking the crowd "You don't really want me to be like that, do you?" And of course, the crowd would respond with a resounding "No!"

Such actions reinforce the idea that now the number one goal of a president is to be entertaining. The idea that politics has completely merged with entertainment is continually reinforced by Trump's public behavior and the media's response to it. Yet few see this as a predictable part of the endlessly aggressive pattern of a Wannabe King. Power makes them more aggressive, not less.

Mistake 7: Treating Moderate Opponents as Enemies

In all of the cases described in this part, opposition to the high-conflict politician is divided. In the case of Hitler, the Social Democrats and other parties in Berlin were constantly squabbling and he took great advantage of that. Both the Nazis and the Communists attacked the Social Democrats and weakened them significantly. If the opposition had somehow joined together with the Moderates, rather than attacking them and each other, they could have stopped him.

In the 2016 primaries for the presidential election in the United States, the progressive wing of the Democratic Party attacked the moderate candidate, Hillary Clinton. And the Democratic Party apparatus apparently manipulated the primary process against the progressive candidate, Bernie Sanders. As described in Chapter 8, if they had stopped fighting earlier, they might have been able to beat Donald Trump.

It appears essential for those who don't want an authoritarian leader to avoid dividing themselves, including attacking moderate opponents as if they are an enemy. Doing so just reinforces the process of weakening Moderates and strengthening the likely authoritarian party.

Mistake 8: Treating the Resisters as Enemies

By the same token, Moderate opponents of a potential authoritarian leader should be careful not to treat the more angry or extreme opponents (Resisters) as enemies. In the Sanders-Clinton primary contest, enough negative things were said about Sanders by the Moderates that many of his followers were pushed away. As we saw, the Moderates needed these votes if they were going to defeat the authoritarian candidate (Trump).

Likewise, it's important not to try to shut down the angry energy of strong opponents for fear of upsetting the Wannabe King's followers. After all, these Loyalists are unlikely to be swayed to vote against their candidate anyway. Their bond is emotional; any logical criticism of their HCP's policies will miss the mark, and any personal criticism of their HCP will just cause the Loyalists to circle the wagons to defend their candidate.

The success of the "resistance" in holding massive peaceful demonstrations after Trump was inaugurated in January 2017 appears to have set limits on his extreme policies in several areas, for a while at least. It also energized the Democratic Party to run many new candidates for office, especially women. Whether on the right or on the left politically, it's important for Moderates to work with the more angry/energized members of their parties in order to block a Wannabe King. The mid-term election in 2018, as described above in Chapter 8, appeared to be a successful coming together of Moderates and Resisters.

Mistake 9: Treating Dropouts as Enemies

In many of these elections, many eligible people avoided voting. If these nonvoters knew then what they know now, they probably would have voted against the Wannabe King. As described in Chapter 8, only 61 percent of eligible voters took part in the 2016 US presidential election. Only 49 percent of millennials voted.[257] Yet these elections will determine their future the most.

It's common for Wannabe Kings to attack the democratic process of elections and to say that they are rigged, in order to discourage their opponents from voting. This apathy helps them get into power. Such a candidate may go on to justify their antidemocratic policies by saying that people don't want to bother with democracy. "It's too much squabbling," as Hitler used to point out about democracy before he took power and became a dictator.[258]

It is tempting for party politicians and campaigners to be highly critical of those who don't vote. However, rather than treating Dropouts as enemies, it may be better to educate them more about the dangers and warning signs of high-conflict politicians. After all, if one is elected without their vote, they will live many more years under a repressive government. All of the stories in this book show how which personality gets elected really does make a difference. It just takes one to alter history, and not for the better. There is a "difference between a Stalin and a Gorbachev," as Steven Pinker has pointed out.[259]

Mistake 10: Treating Loyalists as Enemies

As I have stated before, it's important not to speak negatively of the HCP's Loyalists, as nothing positive is accomplished by doing so. Treating them as enemies just strengthens their bond with the HCP. Be respectful in all your statements about them, just as you would be about any other group. The worst thing is to call them "deplorables," or stupid, or use words like "crush" or "destroy" in relation to them in an election. Even when these are stated to small supportive groups, word gets out. It's better to speak as though your words will show up in the daily news. And sometimes they do!

Conclusion

The takeaway from all of this is that we need to be aware of and respectful of all voters. At the same time, we need to communicate the dangers and deceptions a Wannabe King can present. Part III looks at what we can do to communicate with people about this subject without offending them. There is no benefit for anyone in making enemies while we are trying to prevent another Wannabe King from taking or staying in power.

Part III

HOW TO STOP HIGH-CONFLICT POLITICIANS

Now we have some answers to the three questions I posed in the first chapter:

1. CAN ONE HIGH-CONFLICT POLITICIAN TURN A WELL-FUNCTIONING COMMUNITY—OR NATION—INTO ONE THAT IS EXTREMELY POLARIZED? IF SO, HOW DOES THIS OCCUR?   YES! We have seen this occur in each of the examples I described in Part II. These HCPs start by immediately attacking individuals and groups *within* their communities or countries and teaching their followers to do the same; this includes encouraging individual acts of violence. You might challenge the idea that these Wannabe Kings arose in "well"-functioning communities, but none of the communities or countries described here were as bad off before their Wannabe Kings stepped in as they were afterward. As we have seen, the followers of Wannabe Kings are not usually starving; rather, they are resentful of others succeeding. HCPs know how to charm, con, and manipulate these followers without empathy or remorse.

2. IN A TIME OF PEACE, CAN ONE HIGH-CONFLICT POLITICIAN LEAD A NATION INTO WAR, FAMINE, AND GENOCIDE? IF SO, HOW DOES THIS OCCUR? Again, YES! As the historians have told us, only Hitler wanted World War II. Only Stalin wanted the forced collectivization of Ukraine in a manner that killed approximately four million people. Only Mao wanted the Cultural Revolution that killed approximately seven million people. The advisers around each of these Wannabe Kings tried to stop them, and some paid with their lives.

3. CAN WE STOP HIGH-CONFLICT POLITICIANS BEFORE THEY GET THIS FAR? Again, the answer is YES! But in order to do so, people need to understand the dangers, the deceptions, and the dynamics of high-conflict politicians, and they need to learn how to counteract them in today's high-emotion-media world that favors them. That is what Part III of this book is all about.

The following chapters are addressed to everyone, including candidates for office running against an HCP, people campaigning for someone running against an HCP, and voters who see warning signs of an HCP and want to alert other voters.

This information applies in any election, including as a group leader in the workplace, a community committee like a school board or homeowners association, and a city, state, or national office. The reality is that HCPs want to be "kings" at all levels, but it's easier to see the reality of their patterns at the lower levels, because their Fantasy Crisis Triads don't fit with obvious reality. At national levels its easier for them to create and maintain their fantasies for quite a while, so long as they can keep their realities hidden.

IT'S ALL ABOUT RELATIONSHIPS

Remember it's not about the politics, it's about the personalities; especially when you're dealing with a Wannabe King. This means that your personality matters. As a candidate or campaigner, today's voters aren't going to listen to you, no matter how accurate your reality-based information is and how wonderful your policies are, unless you have a real connection with them. It's all about your positive personality and your relationships.

If our goal is to stop electing narcissists and sociopaths, we have to think differently about our relationships with other voters. We have to pay positive emotional attention to all four groups I have identified: Loyalists (fired-up supporters), Resisters (fired-up opponents), Moderates (voters who are confused or stunned by the HCP's bizarre actions), and Dropouts (people who are disinclined to vote for anyone). We need to create a sense of "us" among all of these groups—or, at the very least, the last three.

Remember, Wannabe Kings are driven to be *always adversarial* and *endlessly aggressive, because of genetic tendencies and/or extreme childhood experiences, which are reinforced (or not) by their cultural environment.* They don't know why they are like this, they don't reflect on their own behavior, and generally, they're unhappy people because their behavior ultimately alienates everyone. Getting angry at an HCP won't change their behavior. Getting organized will.

There are always fewer Loyalists than the total of the other three groups combined. When the other three groups unite, they can always defeat a Wannabe King—provided they do it before the HCP has already seized most of the power.

This means there needs to be no in-fighting. No internal enemies. No attacking other voters (or nonvoters). You can disagree, but not hate each other. I know this approach isn't easy. But I have worked with hundreds of high-conflict situations and I have learned that an assertive, but non-confrontational approach succeeds better than mirroring an HCP's high-conflict behavior.

An HCP will always be better than anyone else at dividing and conquering. But everyone else can be better at uniting and fighting in an effective manner. The electoral process is designed to encourage and support the power of the people.

Reaching Out to Voters

High-conflict politicians know that it's all about their relationships with voters, not their politics. They put almost all of their energy into seducing their voters and dividing the opposition. They pay a lot of attention to their followers by speaking to them publicly almost every day. What they have to say is always the same basic five-part emotional message:

1. *You are special to me. I have a lot of empathy, attention, and respect for you.*

2. *I understand your needs exactly and will help you fulfill them.*

3. *We are victims of our evil enemies, who are taking advantage of you and me.*

4. *I will fight our evil enemies and I need you to fight them with me.*

5. *I am big and strong and energetic, so watch out, world!*

Of course, for narcissists and sociopaths, this is a big con. They don't really care about their voters (although they do like the attention they receive from them) and they don't really understand their voters' needs. But through *emotional repetition in isolation* they are able to convince their voters to become bonded—and often infatuated—with them.

To effectively stop HCPs from getting elected we have to think in terms of relationships—in a similar way to this five-part emotional message—but with a better and more genuine approach. As we've discussed, Wannabe Kings build relationships based on their fantasies, with emotional repetition. We need to build relationships based on *reality*, with positive emotional repetition.

The following relationship skills are the same whether you are a candidate, a campaign staffer or volunteer, or a voter who wishes to influence other voters:

1. GIVE *ALL* VOTERS (AND NONVOTERS) *EMPATHY, ATTENTION*, AND *RESPECT AT ALL TIMES*. In other words, provide a lot of EAR Statements™. (I trademark my methods so that other people won't claim them or change them. But feel free to use them.) EAR Statements include one, two, or all three of these emotional messages:

- I have empathy for you (or care about you and your concerns).
- I will come and pay attention to you.
- I have respect for you.

Be prepared to speak respectfully to every audience—and always speak respectfully *about* everyone—even the HCP (who gets energy from being *disrespected* and doesn't really understand himself anyway).

2. KNOW YOUR AUDIENCE. Yes, it can be good to listen, but what voters really want is someone who already knows and identifies with their interests without them having to explain. Be an "us" from the start. Refer to yourself and your audience as "us" from the start. Talk like an "us" from the start. Don't approach them as strangers you are trying to understand from afar. Approach them as peers who you mostly understand, but from whom you want to hear even more.

3. KNOW THE REALITY OF YOUR ISSUES. Explain your issues as problems you need to solve, rather than people you need to hate or fight.

Say things like *We need to join together to solve our problems, not fight each other.*

Explain that when we simplify issues and turn them into "Us against Them," nothing gets solved and new problems arise.

4. KNOW WHEN TO FIGHT AND WHEN TO COMPROMISE. You can say, *I will fight to be heard and to represent your concerns. But I will also think hard* *about our problems and work hard at creating solutions. I will work with others who want to solve our problems. I will be flexible when flexibility is what's needed. I will compromise when compromise is what's needed. I will fight when fighting is what's needed. And I plan to bring the wisdom to know the difference.*

5. BE STRONG AND ENERGETIC AND POWERFUL. Voters want a relationship with someone who gives the appearance of strength. Voters also want to think of their candidates as winners. Some voters even switch sides close to an election to be on the winning side once they realize which side is going to win. It appears to be part of human nature to want our leaders to be confident, strong, and powerful, and we want to identify with them. Avoid showing weakness or too much doubt. Don't defend yourself too much. If you change your mind, be confident about it. Above all, match the HCP's strength and energy at all times.

Don't spend much time on anyone who you know is already solidly behind the Wannabe King. Treat these people courteously and respect-fully, but don't make them a focus of your energy. On the other hand, everyone will notice if you pay *some* attention to them. The people that really matter in elections are the Moderates, but they like it when you pay respectful attention to the Loyalists—and they do notice.

Here are some more tips in each of these five categories of relationship building:

1. Give All Voters Empathy, Attention, and Respect

The key idea here is that no group of voters wants to be treated in an uncar-ing and disrespectful manner. That is how we get divided and how Wannabe Kings get elected. We have to take an attitude of inclusion toward everyone. We must reject a personally adversarial approach to politics and create a sense of "us" that includes all of us, without creating a sense of "them."

Now, it's clear that this is not going to be easy and that it goes against our biological adversarial heritage. But we also have a biological *cooperative* heritage that we can build on. All human beings are born with the capacity to fight *and* to cooperate.

Our adversarial tendencies can be very helpful. In healthy competition—team sports and business innovations, for example—these tendencies can serve us brilliantly. But in politics, we need to go beyond the adversarial mindset of our ancient Wannabe Kings. We can show empathy, attention, and respect for all—and, in fact, we need to.

ABOUT THE HCP WANNABE KING

High-conflict politicians do not understand themselves and their endlessly aggressive behavior. In other words, it's not their *fault*, but their wiring. We can have empathy for them and their followers, while we work hard to stop them.

Therefore, as much as possible, don't speak *with* any Wannabe King, but speak respectfully *about* them. For example:

> *I understand that _____ can't help himself. He can't stop himself from all the damage he does. He was likely born that way or had a bad childhood. It's sad. But that means we must stop him. All of us must work hard to prevent him from getting elected, or to remove him as soon as possible from office if he is elected. His capacity to be much more dangerous with more power must motivate us to stop him now. We must put our energy into organizing to stop him, rather than just being angry at him every day.*

LOYALISTS

Don't waste time trying to persuade hard-core Wannabe King supporters. They are true believers who will follow their candidate wherever they go and support them no matter what they do. They have an emotional bond that is almost impossible to break. But you should say "Hi" to them at some point in a campaign to show respect.

There is a subgroup of Loyalists who may actually be open to rejecting the HCP but won't say so publicly. They will listen closely to what you say about the HCP—if you are calm, respectful, and energized.

Both of these groups of Loyalists need to hear that you spoke respectfully *about them* and *about their candidate*.

Nevertheless, give the remaining three groups the lion's share of your time, attention, empathy, and respect.

RESISTERS

These voters are the most energized and passionate, and in many ways, the key to success in getting out the vote against a Wannabe King. Feel free to empathize with their anger and their fears. Let them know that you see the dangers the high-conflict politician poses and that we all need to fight the HCP together.

But let them know that they also need to empathize with the Moderates and not make enemies of them. The key to success in blocking or removing a Wannabe King is in getting the Resisters and the Moderates to work together.

The Resisters may be key to providing the energy it takes to get the Mild Moderates to become Energized Moderates, so teach them about the 4-way split that HCPs cause and explain that you can't allow the HCP to succeed at this.

You also need to communicate to them that primary election battles between Resisters and Moderates of the same political party need to end well before any general election to give the two factions time to reunite. In addition to these two groups, the Dropouts can potentially oppose the Wannabe King. All three need to unite well before the general election.

Psychologically people cannot overcome high-intensity conflicts within their own group in a short period of time, if ever. This is the mistake that Bernie Sanders and Hillary Clinton made in the Democratic primaries in 2016. This is also why Ronald Reagan promoted the "Eleventh Commandment":

> The personal attacks against me during the primary finally became so heavy that the state Republican chairman, Gaylord Parkinson, postulated what he called the Eleventh Commandment: Thou shalt not speak ill of any fellow Republican. It's a rule I followed during that campaign and have ever since.[260]

In other words, let the HCP make all the personal attacks—they won't be able to restrain themselves. As Michelle Obama, wife of former President Obama, has said: "There was a motto Barack and I tried to live by, and I offered it that night from the stage: *When they go low, we go high.*"[261] You can then point out the inappropriateness of this in a respectful way. After all, the political culture needs to change if we are going to stop having Wannabe Kings run in so many elections.

Everyone needs to know that personal attacks are inappropriate in solving modern problems. Even if some heated moments do occur in primaries, they need to be healed before any general election against a high-conflict politician.

Explain to everyone in each of the three anti-HCP camps that this is more important than any ideological differences among the three groups. Remind them that the single most important goal in the election is to defeat the Wannabe King. Also remind them that if an endlessly aggressive HCP wins the election, life will be much worse for everyone.

MODERATES

The Mild Moderates are usually the Evil Establishment in the eyes of the Wannabe King and his followers. They are usually subjected to the most intense personal attacks and are usually caught by surprise by how vicious they can be. Because the Wannabe King sees them as the ones in power, they make them the focus of their unwanted attention.

A good example of this dynamic is what happened in the Republican primaries before the 2016 presidential election. In these primaries, Donald Trump personally attacked each of the other candidates in an emotionally repetitive way that was incredibly effective and memorable. He attached an emotionally disparaging adjective to each of his key opponents: Lyin' Ted Cruz. Little Marco Rubio. Low Energy Jeb Bush. And so on.

Trump then repeated these monikers over and over again during the Republican primaries on TV and to his followers at rallies. He effectively immobilized his opponents because they could not figure out how to respond. This was not a skill they had developed up to this point in their long political careers.

It almost seemed as if Trump had adopted the lesson Hitler claimed to have learned in the 1920s: "[U]nleash a veritable barrage of lies and slander against whatever adversary seems most dangerous, until the nerves of the attacked person break down."[262]

Moderates must stick together and speak up in their own defense, such as with BIFF Responses that provide confident information rather than helplessness in response, as I will describe in Chapter 13.

DROPOUTS

Many voters drop out for a variety of reasons. In the general presidential election of 2016, only 61.4 percent of eligible adults voted according to the Pew Research organization. The percentage of African-Americans who voted (59.6 percent) was down from 66.6 percent in 2012. Slightly fewer than 50 percent of Millennials, Hispanic Americans, and Asian Americans voted, although the percentage of Millennials who voted was slightly higher than in 2012 (49.4 percent, up from 46.4 percent).[263]

In terms of communicating with this group, it should help to empathize with their frustration with elections, their belief that their vote doesn't matter, and their busy lives. There's no reason to disrespect them. Instead, the message needs to be (at the very least) that these are extraordinary circumstances—when a high-conflict politician runs for office, the stakes for democracy are much higher. Communicating the dangers of such a candidate are essential. If possible, communicate how it may directly affect them and that you care about their futures as well as your own.

2. Know Your Audience

In building a relationship with anyone, you need to give something of yourself to connect with them. Find out what you have in common (in advance, if possible). If you can, tell a short story that shows you identify with them. It's fine to laugh at yourself or share an embarrassing moment *as long as* it shows that you are similar to them, not different.

Don't start your connection with a new group of people by telling them about a policy, abstract issue, or position they should take. Start by connecting to them *as a person.* Only after you have made this connection are people going to listen to your ideas and logical information. No matter how much of a hurry you are in, you need to connect *as a person*; otherwise, nothing else that you say will matter.

If you can identify what their particular fears and frustrations are, it can be very helpful to address these. Remember, fear and anger are the emotion high-conflict politicians use to form their strongest connections with their followers—especially their true believers.

Try to focus on people's fears and how to address them. You can say that you share their anger and frustration with an *issue,* but be careful not to make another person or group the enemy. In fact, when you can, say that focusing anger on another person or group may feel good for a moment, but it won't solve today's modern, complex problems.

You might even mention how Senator John McCain handled a voter's anger at Barack Obama during the 2008 presidential election when they were running against each other: a voter in the audience at a Town Hall meeting said that Obama was an Arab, implying that he wasn't born in America and therefore shouldn't be allowed to run for President. But McCain immediately took the microphone and came to Obama's defense:

> "No ma'am, no ma'am," McCain said as the conservative crowd booed the Republican nominee. "He's a decent family man, citizen, that I just happen

to have disagreements with on fundamental issues. That's what this campaign is all about."[264]

3. Know the Reality of Your Issues

Focus on explaining issues and what *really* needs to be done to alleviate people's fears regarding these issues, such as investing in a specific solution or restraining individuals, companies, or agencies of government (depending on your political perspective). Promote positive solutions, such as to healthcare and education and infrastructure.

Avoid making a person or group into the enemy. Don't focus on the fantasy hero, tempting as it is. Focus on the fantasy crisis and how it's not a crisis. Focus on real problems and real solutions.

Take an educational approach to your audience, but keep your message simple and repetitive. They will appreciate having knowledge that they didn't have before. You might even bond with them by making a simple chant or meme out of your factual information.

For example, research shows that immigrants to America actually work harder than the average citizen, work undesirable hours, and work undesirable jobs. This is shown by a study reported in the *Washington Post* in 2017, which reached the following conclusions:

Immigrants are substantially more likely to work unusual hours than U.S.-born workers.

Immigrants play a particularly large role filling odd hour jobs in several key sectors of the economy.

Female immigrants are considerably more likely to work unusual hours than U.S.-born women.

Immigrants and U.S.-born workers who work unusual hours are often not competing for the same jobs.[265]

In addition, research spanning thirty-six years shows that on the whole, immigrants commit fewer crimes than US citizens. This includes both legal immigrants and undocumented immigrants.

According to data from the study, a large majority of the areas have many more immigrants today than they did in 1980 and fewer violent crimes. The Marshall Project extended the study's data up to 2016, showing that crime fell more often than it rose even as immigrant populations grew almost across the board.[266]

So with this knowledge, anyone can come up with the following chant:

Immigrants Work Hard

and

Cause Less Crime

This is *factual information with emotional repetition* because it's a chant that includes key words like "work hard" and "less crime." The more often such a chant is repeated with emotional intensity, the more likely it is to enter people's brains and get them to remember it, just like a TV commercial.

4. Know When to Fight and When to Compromise

High-conflict politicians only know how to fight because they are endlessly adversarial. You can point that out. Effective politicians know that compromise is also necessary at times (unlike in the fantasies of fictional TV shows and movies). The skill of compromise is what our nation was founded on and how all laws since then have been made. That's why there is a division of the duties of the branches of government built into most democratic countries' constitutions.

You can point out that high-conflict politicians have difficulty compromising because they are stuck with all-or-nothing thinking, which doesn't allow them to compromise, even when doing so benefits people. You can point out that you (or your candidate) will compromise when it makes sense and fight when that makes sense. You want someone smart and creative, not someone stuck in a rut who tries to solve all problems by being a bully.

5. Be Strong and Energetic and Powerful

This is surprisingly important to all voters. Over and over again in examining the appeal of "strongman" rulers, voters say that they feel safer and more secure with a strong leader. *This appears to be more important than any particular policy and any particular party.*

I believe that this goes back to the early days of human history, when people really did need a physically strong leader to protect them from many physical dangers.

Conclusion

Focusing on building relationships with today's voters is essential. That's how narcissistic and sociopathic Wannabe Kings seduce their followers. Use emotions, but use positive emotions. Don't waste time and energy on bad-mouthing the HCP. Just mention him (or her) in passing, and focus on issues. Focus on the fantasy crisis issue and explain why it's not a crisis but perhaps a problem to solve. Focus on real problems and how they will address your listeners' needs.

SCREEN OUT NARCISSISTS AND SOCIOPATHS

F
ew people really know about the existence of these high-conflict personalities, how dangerous they can be, and how deceptive they are.

If someone doesn't know about HCPs and their surprisingly obvious
warning signs, they are apt to get fooled and possibly even make things
worse. They may become seduced into becoming a *Negative Advocate*—an
enabler—for a narcissistic and/or sociopathic HCP Wannabe King.

Now that *you* understand the basics of these HCP politicians, you can
start teaching their patterns to other people.

In my experience, people are motivated to understand the personalities
of the public people in their lives and the private people around them. I often
hear that people wish they knew this information months or years ago.

Always Adversarial, Endlessly Aggressive

The most fundamental behavior of high-conflict people (HCPs) is the same
anywhere: they are *always adversarial,* even when they are sounding reasonable or being seductive. They are willing to attack anyone, including

those close to them—family, friends, loyal colleagues, people in positions of authority. This widespread, predictable, adversarial pattern of HCPs is in-born and/or learned from early childhood experiences and influenced by the person's culture.

HCPs shock most people with how *endlessly aggressive* they are, even at times when most other people would back off from adversarial behavior and try to collaborate as peers. Unfortunately, in many conflicts, the most endlessly aggressive person prevails (at least temporarily) over those who get tired of being adversarial themselves. This is the advantage that HCPs have over everyone else. They have an *enduring pattern* that can keep going and going and going.

This is how Donald Trump beat out sixteen other candidates in the Republican primaries in 2016. He never stopped being *personally aggressive*. He personally attacked each candidate as a human being, while they tried to look reasonable, logical, and collegial and were repeatedly caught off-guard.

Similarly, those who work and live around an HCP are usually not prepared for someone this endlessly aggressive and therefore often defer to them because it's easier in the moment. *Sure, let Joe be in charge; he wants it so badly.* They don't realize that when someone seems *extreme* about wanting to be in charge, this is a warning sign of an HCP. This may be the exact wrong person to lead the team and people need to realize this.

In elections, three sets of people can screen out HCPs. Here is my advice to each group:

- **Committees that select and nominate candidates within political parties:** Don't pick, support, or encourage an HCP candidate, for any reason, under any circumstances. You will *always* regret it.

- **Volunteers and paid organizers who campaign for a candidate:** Don't work or campaign for an HCP candidate, under any circumstances, for any reason. Sooner or later, they will turn on you and shock you with their vicious attacks.

- **Voters:** Don't vote for an HCP candidate, under any circumstances, for any reason. They will do everything they can to ruin democracy and rule of law—and they will do their best to destroy everyone and everything that stands in their way.

Early Warning Signs

Keep in mind that people with personality disorders have a narrower pattern of behavior than the average person. In the *Diagnostic and Statistical Manual of Mental Health Professionals* (the DSM-5), this is described as an *enduring pattern that is pervasive* across many settings in the person's life. This essentially means that they aren't flexible and don't change. Therefore, their behavior is generally *more obvious and predictable* than that of the average person. This is equally true for people with high-conflict personalities, whether they have a personality disorder or not.

Let's review the warning signs from Chapter 1. A Wannabe King will have many or all of the following attributes. The more powerful the office the person aspires to, the more extreme these traits are likely to be.

HIGH-CONFLICT PERSONALITY KEY TRAITS

1. Targets of Blame

2. All-or-nothing thinking

3. Unmanaged emotions

4. Extreme behaviors

Most Wannabe Kings will also have some or all of the following personality traits:

NARCISSISTIC PERSONALITY TRAITS

1. Drive to be superior

2. Grandiose ideas

3. Fantasies of unlimited power

4. Lack of empathy

ANTISOCIAL (SOCIOPATHIC) PERSONALITY TRAITS

1. Drive to dominate

2. Deceitful (lying and conning)

3. Highly aggressive

4. Lack of remorse

Spotting High-Conflict Politician Patterns

There are three methods for spotting these patterns of high-conflict politicians—and for pointing them out to others. I'll describe the WEB Method® in this chapter. The other two are in the Appendices. Appendix A is "40 Predictable Behaviors of HCPs," and Appendix B is the "High-Conflict Politician Scorecard." Those are both self-explanatory.

Using the WEB Method

The WEB Method involves paying attention to an HCP's *words,* your *emotions, and* the HCP's *behavior.* (For a detailed description of this method, see my book *5 Types of People Who Can Ruin Your Life: Identifying and Dealing with Narcissists, Sociopaths and Other High-Conflict Personalities.*)

THEIR WORDS

High-conflict politicians are especially easy to spot with this method because they say (and often write or tweet) so many words. Indeed, every HCP described in Part II of this book was (or is) known for speaking *five to ten times as much* as other politicians. This is probably because of their narcissistic tendencies, which demand excessive attention and admiration.

Look for words that show a lot of the following:

BLAMING:

- *Once again, it's the fault of the [Jews, kulaks, drug addicts, the elite, the establishment, Muslims, Mexicans, Republicans, Democrats, etc.]!*
- *We're in this mess because of the decisions of the last administration.*
- *You can't trust _____, and they're right over there!*

They also never apologize, never take responsibility for making bad decisions, and never reevaluate their past actions, decisions, or practices.

ALL-OR-NOTHING THINKING:

- *It's us against them!*
- *It's ALL _____'s fault!*
- *Their way is a total disaster and must be completely shut down.*
- *I will do the best job anyone has ever done in this position.*

- *The person now holding this position has done the worst job in the history of the country.*
- *I choose the best people to work for me. And, of course, only the best people vote for me.*
- *Every single thing you just said is a lie.*

UNMANAGED OR INTENSE EMOTIONS:

- *You make me ashamed to be a citizen of this great nation. You know what I want to do right now? Come over and slug you in your ugly, stupid face.*
- *The prior chair of this committee was totally incompetent!*
- *You're a disgrace! You should be stripped of all your awards!*
- *HOW DARE YOU! Apologize to these good people right now!*
- *When I look at what my opponent has done to this country, I want to throw up.*

EXTREME BEHAVIOR OR THREATS:

- *I will eliminate most of the programs of the last administration.*
- *I will invest all of our resources in this wonderful new project.*
- *We have to do it exactly the way we have always done in the past, without any change.*
- *It will be easy to win a war on this issue. I know exactly what we need to do.*
- *The answer is simple: lock him up and throw away the key.*

OTHER FREQUENT WORDS OF NARCISSISTIC LEADERS:

- *I know what everyone here needs to do.*
- *I have a plan, but I'm not going to tell you what it is until you elect me.*
- *The other side is a bunch of losers.*
- *I will be better at doing _____ than anyone who ever held this position.*
- *You'll look back and see how totally right I was and totally wrong you were.*

OTHER FREQUENT WORDS OF SOCIOPATHIC LEADERS:

- *I will crush _____ [you, the opposition, anyone who questions me, our enemies].*
- *We will dominate _____ [the opposition, our neighbors, the establishment].*
- *This group of _____ is a bunch of insects who don't deserve to live.*
- *They are trying to control us—but we will destroy them.*
- *Politics is always war—and we must win the war by any means necessary.*
- *My opponent is so corrupt, you won't believe it! His tax returns belong in fantasyland!*

YOUR EMOTIONS

Reflect on how you feel in your relationship with the politician. Get used to paying attention to any extreme feelings you may have.

EXTREMELY NEGATIVE:

- Do you feel afraid, vulnerable, or anxious when they speak?
- Do you feel that, if this person gets into power, you will be personally and politically doomed?
- Do you feel demoralized and helpless when you hear their policies?
- Do you feel like the politician is going to pull the rug out from under us?
- Do you feel angry?
- When you hear the person speak, or see their face, do you want to scream?
- Do you feel afraid to speak negatively in public about the person?
- Are you afraid that if you let people know how you feel about the person, you will be viciously attacked?

EXTREMELY POSITIVE:

- Does the person feel or seem too good to be true?
- Do you feel infatuated with them?

- Do you just love them and think they would be the best person who has ever held the office?
- Do you feel compelled to follow them or listen to them?

THEIR BEHAVIOR

Of course, no one trait or incident creates a certainty about one's personality and future behavior. But all put together, you may see a pattern that you don't like in a candidate.

- Does the person do negative things that 90 percent of people would never do, such as throw things across the room at people?
- Do they spend a lot of time denying things that others say they did?
- Do they spend a lot of time criticizing people on their team?
- Do they attack both close friends and distant foes?
- Do they pretend (or claim) to have experience, talents, or abilities that they don't have?
- Do they lie a lot?

Jamming Your Radar

HCP Wannabe Kings engage many subtle techniques of distraction and deception while they are seducing their Loyalists. Here are a few:

1. Straying from the topic or jumping repeatedly from one topic to another
2. Saying things that make no sense at all (though they might—or might not—seem to at first)
3. Telling voters how much they care about them or even how much they love them
4. Telling voters how much they will do for them—but in uselessly general, nonspecific terms (*You're going to be so happy and successful!*)
5. Promising voters things that are very specific, utterly impossible, and transparently false (*When I'm president, every single one of you will become a millionaire! I guarantee it!*)
6. Promising voters how great things will be, but never saying how they will achieve it (*We will become the greatest power in the history of the world! Why? Because that's where I'll take us.*)

7. Insisting that they and the voters share the same concerns (*What you care about is exactly what I care about.*)

8. Proclaiming that they are just like the people they are speaking to (*You and me—we're just the same, aren't we? What's good for you is what's good for me. And we both know how the world really works, don't we?*)

Some Important Reminders

Knowing the warning signs of HCPs can help you avoid getting into many bad situations. It's worth learning these predictable patterns and teaching them to others.

However, I have a few words of caution. Remember, you're not diagnosing narcissists and sociopaths—or any other mental disorder. You're just learning ways to protect yourself and your community from the *possibility* of one or more high-conflict personalities.

Don't tell people that you are certain about someone else's personality. Just say something like this, as one example:

> *I have some serious concerns about so-and-so, and I won't be [selecting him as a candidate], [working for him as a candidate], or [voting for him]. He seems to have a lot of all-or-nothing thinking, and he seems preoccupied with blaming other people. To me, these are key warning signs that he won't be a reasonable decision-maker and will be stuck fighting unnecessarily with people, when there are important issues that need attention instead.*

If you use phrasing similar to this, you can warn people without being seen as judging their personality unfairly or diagnosing someone with a mental health issue. Remember, a high-conflict personality (HCP) is *not* a mental health diagnosis but a description of how someone behaves in a conflict. So, if you feel compelled to say that you think a candidate's personality is truly dangerous and want to say why, you could say this:

> *I have concerns that he has a high-conflict personality and will escalate our community/state/nation into war, because that's what HCPs often do. They are always adversarial and endlessly aggressive and can't stop themselves. So it's better that we stop him now—by not electing him.*

You may want to practice that with friends before you say it to strangers just to get used to the idea and to build your confidence. Remember, your sense of strength and confidence can be very appealing.

Conclusion

Screening out HCPs from being elected won't be very hard once a lot of people realize their dangers and their patterns. One of the hardest things for people to realize about these HCPs is that they really do lack empathy and remorse, and they really attack people for no good reason. The bad behavior is about them and not about the person they're attacking. In politics, it's about the political issue, it's about the personality. Pay attention to the patterns of behavior, don't be misled by what they're talking about. Would 90 percent of people say and do what they are saying and doing? Would you ever say or do that? Asking ourselves these questions will help everyone in preventing HCPs from getting into dangerous positions of power over us.

EXPOSE THEIR FANTASY
CRISIS TRIADS

People like understanding what is going on in the world and they really like being able to spot patterns in other people's behavior.

Some people may recall the moment in the 2016 Republican primary debates when Governor Chris Christie criticized Senator Marco Rubio for having a *pattern* of just repeating his talking points in response to other candidate's comments and questions.

> Mr. Christie had instructed the audience to listen for what he dismissively called the "memorized 25-second speech," adding, with a twist of the knife, that it was "exactly what his advisers gave him."
>
> . . .
>
> When it was his turn to reply, Mr. Rubio—inexplicably—seemed to fulfill Mr. Christie's prediction, repeating the main idea of that same memorized-sounding speech about Mr. Obama. Almost word for word.
>
> "This notion that Barack Obama doesn't know what he's doing is just not true," Mr. Rubio said. "He knows exactly what he's doing."
>
> Mr. Christie pounced. "There it is," he said icily, turning to Mr. Rubio and jabbing his finger at him. "There it is, everybody."[267]

The crowd then cheered Mr. Christie. They enjoyed learning about someone's narrow pattern of behavior and then seeing it demonstrated right before their eyes.

From my years of experience teaching people about high-conflict personality patterns, almost everyone likes learning about personality patterns that they can recognize and behaviors that they can expect in the future. Most people will appreciate learning about the narrow pattern of the Fantasy Crisis Triad. Once someone learns about it, it's hard not to notice it when high-conflict politicians speak. But while this can be enjoyable, it's also very serious.

The key to explaining this is to focus primarily on the fantasy crisis itself more than the fantasy villain or fantasy hero. The fantasy hero and fantasy villain are mostly about two tribes and the attack-and-defend adversarial process. The fantasy crisis, however, is about reality. Facts and analysis usually clear up whether something is genuinely a crisis or a problem that needs to be solved.

But let's start out by looking at why we shouldn't emphasize criticizing the fantasy hero or defending the fantasy villain.

Don't Emotionally Attack the Fantasy Hero

One of the big mistakes that many fact-focused politicians and their supporters make in response to a high-conflict politician is to point out how ridiculous he is. These disparaging comments are what makes the news, but they actually *strengthen* the HCPs relationship with his followers.

Remember that the high-conflict politician has taught his followers that they are the victims of a powerful, evil group of people—his Targets of Blame—namely, you and your candidate, party, race, organization, nation, and so on. The HCP teaches people that there are two groups or tribes: Us and Them. Their tribe has a heroic leader, the Wannabe King. At the core of their tribe are their Loyalists.

When you attack their leader, they feel that you are attacking all of them. From the start of their campaigns (if not well before), high-conflict politicians train their followers to respond angrily to their opponents, by yelling at them, chanting about them at their rallies, trolling them on the internet, and so on.

An example of this was described in 2009–2010 when the Affordable Care Act for healthcare considered by Congress was being presented to the

American people. At one point, Alaska governor Sarah Palin dramatically said that the ACA would have "death panels" to decide who got healthcare and who didn't. This was not true and was corrected in the media. Yet here is what happened next:

> But the correction actually backfired among Palin supporters. . . . After receiving the correction, they became *more* likely to believe that the Affordable Care Act contained death panels. Ironically, the correction intensified their original belief. The study suggests that if members of an out-group support some proposition, their very support might entrench the preexisting beliefs of the in-group.[268]

This happened because the group had an emotional bond with a leader, rather than a logical, information-focused bond. They got energy from being attacked and responding together. *This proves to them that they are on the same team as their loved leader!*

This is the strongest human bond there is: joining together in battle *against an enemy*, working together *against the enemy*, while also sharing beliefs *about the enemy*.

In this case, Sarah Palin ran for vice president in 2008 as a Republican and, after losing, she built quite a following by waging war against the establishment of the Republican party as being the cause of many of her fantasy crises. For a time, she was considered a contender for president in 2012, but she eventually demonstrated her lack of experience and her inability to handle real problems. By 2011, even Roger Ailes, head of Fox News, said "she's an idiot!"[269]

In their book, *New Power,* this is what Jeremy Heimans and Henry Timms had to say about the way that Donald Trump inspired his followers:

> Trump became the leader of a vast, decentralized social media army who took cues from him—and who in turn fed Trump new narratives and lines of attack. It was a deeply symbiotic relationship. . . . He drove the intensity of his crowd not by insisting that they read his talking points, but by empowering them to activate around his values. Think of him as a *Platform Strongman,* mastering new power techniques to achieve authoritarian ends.[270]

The paradox here is that the more Trump is attacked, the more it strengthens his bond with his followers. It's not just that they cheer him, but they also—using social media—share a common task in defending him online with the emotional intensity of an army.

People are often shocked at the power of the negative feedback they get from Trump's followers in response to minor criticisms in social media postings or online news articles or opinion pieces. Pointing out their leader's lack of knowledge feeds them with an opportunity for a war-like response. Here's a dramatic example:

> Strikingly, according to these social media analysts, the moment during the campaign that expanded Trump's social media following the most was his campaign's supposed nadir: the release of the *Access Hollywood* tape in which he boasted about pussy-grabbing. This moment, with much of the country lined up against him, caused his supporters to rally around him like at no other time in the race.[271]

The result of all of this, is that emotionally attacking the high-conflict leader

- Reinforces his narcissistic claim that he is being treated unfairly by his opponents, and needs to be defended.
- Strengthens his followers' bond with him.
- Energizes his followers to fight for him.
- May make *you* look bad to the Dropouts.
- Changes no one's thinking, as it isn't about thinking—it's about emotional bonds between high-conflict leaders and followers.

Don't Focus on Emotionally Defending the Fantasy Villain

Since the high-conflict politician has turned the election into an intensely adversarial contest between Us and Them, when you intensely defend your candidate, you are fitting into his construct of the crisis. You feed the highly emotional contest, which reinforces blocked thinking and emotional reactions. It becomes about attack and defend rather than about useful information.

In addition, the high-conflict politician will *always* be better at attack and defend, because that is all they do and it is often a lifetime skill—a narrow pattern of behavior.

Rather than focusing on defending your candidate (the Wannabe King's fantasy villain), simply explain your candidate's skills, experience, and goals.

Then, respond to the substantive attacks with useful information, often about the fact that there is no crisis and that you have information about real problems and real solutions.

An Informative Approach about the Fantasy Crisis Triad

What I am recommending here is what I have found works over and over again in legal disputes opposing a high-conflict personality. Take an informative approach, rather than an adversarial one, to teaching the Fantasy Crisis Triad to others.

Explain that the HCP politician appears to have a *pattern* of believing in misinformation about this situation, just because it *feels* true. But the feeling comes from high-emotion media and emotional repetition rather than factual information. The real problem is that this politician appears to have a Fantasy Crisis Triad.

For example:

Mr. _____ is misinformed, which is sad and dangerous.

He appears to believe that there is a terrible crisis involving [immigrants committing lots of crimes] [unfair trade with our neighboring countries] [minorities in our country who are out to get us] [some other terrible threat to our way of life].

However, the reality is that good research tells us that [immigrants cause less crime than natural-born citizens] [we don't have unfair trade with our neighboring countries, but instead, when you include services, we have a trade surplus ...] [today's minorities are more like us than different from us—for example ...] [the world we actually live in is much better or safer than the one Mr. _____ is making up]. In other words, there isn't a terrible crisis. Instead [there's a problem to solve, but it's not a crisis; there are methods, policies, people in place already addressing it] or [it's a total fantasy and unrelated to any real problem today].

BIFF Responses

Here is a simple way to remember how anyone can respond to one of the HCP's false statements. It involves being *brief, informative, friendly,* and *firm*

(BIFF). This is a method I developed for the High Conflict Institute that we have taught to thousands of people over the past twelve years. It has helped them deal with family disputes, workplace conflicts, and legal cases more calmly and productively. It really works to take the steam out of false or hostile statements.

BIFF responses can be used to effectively respond to newspaper articles and letters to the editor; Facebook posts, tweets, and other social media posts; angry or argumentative e-mails; and in-person discussions. They are especially useful in dealing with an HCP's surrogates and Negative Advocates.

SAMPLE BIFF RESPONSES

Here are three examples of hostile messages you might receive from an HCP or one of their supporters, and some sample BIFF responses you or someone else might use:

ON IMMIGRATION

Fearful Citizen:

Mexicans are pouring into this country. They are rapists, criminals, and murderers. Your candidate supports a totally open border and eliminating immigration enforcement. Don't you care about your country? Don't you care if citizens get killed?

You:

I agree with you that not everyone should be admitted into our country or given citizenship. That's why my candidate doesn't support a totally open border or eliminating immigration enforcement. You've been misinformed, because my candidate supports a moderate immigration policy. We want to reward hard work and give reasonable immigrants a pathway to citizenship like we have always done. Lots of research shows that immigrants work hard and cause less crime.

The highlighted phrases in this example, and later ones, can be repeated over and over again in responding to many different hostile comments or emails on the same general topic. The more people repeat the same phrases, the more power they develop.

ON TRADE

Fearful Citizen:

Trade agreements are ruining us! The ones the previous administrations have nego-tiated are the worst ever. They sent jobs overseas and destroyed our manufacturing. Don't you care about the future of our economy and our workers? You must be a socialist!!

Campaigner:

I agree that our trade agreements are important because they can save us money and expand markets for us. You have been misinformed: the previous deals are not the worst ever and have been successful in many areas of business. Our employment levels are high now and our manufacturing is at an all-time high, although there are fewer jobs because of automation. Of course, trade deals can always be improved, but taking an all-or-nothing approach and throwing them out risks alienating our trade partners and destabilizing economies. As most employers will tell you, a stable world economy *needs* stable trade agreements.

In this example, more could have been said, but keeping it relatively brief is better. Not everything has to be replied to, such as the socialist comment. It's best to avoid name-calling while making information the focus.

ON CITY POLITICS

City Attorney:

You're the mayor and supposed to protect the city from bad pension plan agreements. But you have committed fraud in not protecting our citizens and our budget by allowing a bad pension deal for the city. Someday your fraudulent ways will be exposed. I am telling everyone I talk to at public meetings your fraud is ruining us! Your false and misleading statements will be exposed!

Mayor:

I appreciate the city attorney's concern about the city's finances. We are in a hard situ-ation and I share those concerns. Several auditors have looked into some poor pension decisions that were made before my time, and none of them have reached the con-clusion that they were fraudulent or criminal. So I hope you will join me, rather than focusing on the past, to focus on the future.

Rather than get defensive, the mayor has provided useful information and remained respectful.

GENERAL BAD INTENT

High-conflict politician:

My opponent has only two interests: raising your taxes and breaking up your family. She'll deny this, though, because she's a compulsive liar.

You:

My candidate has no interest in raising your taxes or breaking up your family. She has made several efforts to support struggling families, such as her _____ initiative. You have been misinformed. She believes that the wealthy should pay their fair share of taxes, which should ease the burden for middle class families, unlike the tax cuts of the previous administration. Her opponent likes to make all-or-nothing statements like this to grab your attention. Next time he makes a statement about my candidate, watch for the all-or-nothing statements that provide no useful information.

BIFF Responses get easier and easier as you get familiar with each part: they need to be brief, informative, friendly, and firm. They don't engage with the emotional side of the other person's statement but focus on facts. When they aren't triggered into their emotions, most people are interested in facts and will listen. This avoids the escalation of an emotional back-and-forth, while actually educating people about real life. Information turns fantasy crises into problems to solve and eliminates problems that don't exist.

Conclusion

Responses that provide information rather than emotional retorts will defuse an HCP or his follower's upset energy and sometimes even makes others more open to dealing with solving a problem. It's also a way to simply end an unproductive conversation, which you may need to do if you are dealing with a riled-up Loyalist for an HCP—or the HCP himself or herself. For lots of examples and a more detailed explanation, see my book: *BIFF: Quick Responses to High Conflict People, Their Personal Attacks, Hostile Emails and Social Media Meltdowns.*

BE AS ASSERTIVE AS
HCPs ARE AGGRESSIVE

L et's start with what *not* to do. One common (and natural) response to
very aggressive behavior is to become passive—to defer to the aggressive
person. With an HCP, however, *never* respond with passivity. If you do, they
will trample you, humiliate you, attempt to destroy you, and call you weak.
They will never pause in their attacks, even for a moment. Some literally *never*
stop for as long as they live. As we have seen over and over again, with more
time and power, they always become more dangerously aggressive, not less.

Another common (and equally natural) response to an HCP's over-the-
top aggression is similar aggressiveness. But with an HCP, *never* respond
with aggression either, even for a moment. If you do, then from that moment
on, they will paint you as angry, crazy, destructive, and potentially violent—
and themselves as sane, reasonable, and level-headed. They will show the
world a video clip of your aggressive response thousands of times.

Yet another common (and natural response) to an HCP's highly aggressive attacks is to ignore them. But if you refuse to respond, the HCP will
attack you for running away, for being a coward, or for trying to hide from
"the truth." They will relentlessly repeat these baseless attacks.

Here's an example of trying to ignore a high-conflict personal attack during an election.

Swiftboating

In the 2004 United States presidential election, John Kerry was running for president against George W. Bush. Kerry touted his experience in the Vietnam War as a Navy officer in charge of sailors on several Swift boats patrolling in the Mekong River Delta, for which he received several medals. After the war he became a congressman and then senator.

During the 2004 campaign, a book was published by a group of sailors called the Swift Boat Veterans for Truth (SBVT), which claimed that Kerry's military service was dishonest and unpatriotic, and that he should not have received his medals. John Kerry considered these claims so absurd that he assumed that no one would pay attention to them. As a result, his campaign did not respond to them. Then, suddenly, the accusations exploded in the news with lots of repetition, as though they were all true.

In time, journalists took a close look at these claims and interviewed numerous military people who were involved around him. It became clear that these claims against Kerry were almost completely false. A connection was also discovered between the SBVT and a lawyer for the Bush campaign, who promptly left the campaign. As one journalist said at the time:

> The bottom line? Mr. Kerry has stretched the truth here and there, but earned his decorations. And the Swift Boat Veterans, contradicted by official records and virtually everyone who witnessed the incidents, are engaging in one of the ugliest smears in modern U.S. politics.[272]

Unfortunately, Mr. Kerry did not respond to these allegations against him until they gained significant coverage during the campaign—possibly contributing to his loss of the election.

Since then, *Swiftboating* has become the term for a dishonest smear attack during a political campaign that often goes without a response.

The Assertive Approach

The best approach—perhaps the *only* approach—that works with a high-conflict politician is an assertive one, in which you actively protect yourself (or the candidate you support); match the HCP's energy, but *not* their vindictiveness; focus on the facts; and do so without attacking or trying to destroy the Wannabe King.

The key is to present *only* factual, accurate information, and to do so in a way that is focused, clear, and strong (even forceful), but calm.

Always present this information as soon as possible after an HCP's attack. When possible, present it in the same forum—for example, in the same newspaper, in the same debate, or on the same social media site.

Its fine to be very brief, but you *must* respond as quickly as possible so that your factual information follows quickly on the heels of the HCP's misinformation—and so the HCP doesn't have a lot of time to spread their lies and have them grow.

At all times, be just as energetic as the HCP. Show strength and confidence while providing useful information. Stay matter-of-fact and calm. Your accurate, helpful information and your demeanor are your strengths. Both clearly differentiate you from the HCP and their surrogates.

When you take such an assertive approach, the HCP and their followers will do everything they can to confuse you, upset you, or make you angry. They will call you names. They will accuse you of saying things you did not. They will claim that you committed some imaginary sin or crime. Their goal is to emotionally rattle you in the hope that you will misspeak or lose your cool and stop looking reasonable.

All of this means that you must do your homework and be accurate at all times. The HCP will seize on the slightest error or inconsistency and use it to "prove" that you are a sleazy, untrustworthy liar who just wants to hoodwink everyone.

Actually, no matter what you say and do, the HCP may denounce you as a total liar—or crook, or paid sycophant—anyway. Remember, they are *endlessly aggressive* and can't stop themselves. Respond to these accusations with even more factual, accurate information. Or simply repeat your prior factual points once more.

The reason this is successful is that you look reasonable, and not wild and angry and dangerous. As a result, it's hard to paint you as an extremist, so you won't alienate anyone. Also, the assertive approach makes it harder for you to be seen as a fantasy villain or Target of Blame.

Be Everywhere

When campaigning against an HCP Wannabe King, you are always in an uphill battle. Most HCPs are intuitively media savvy and will flood every possible medium with the same false and emotionally seductive messages, repeating them endlessly.

So, if you can, be just as present as the Wannabe King on every medium they use. Remember, Hitler, Stalin, Mao, McCarthy, Berlusconi, Trump, and many other HCPs succeeded significantly because their faces and messages were *everywhere*.

If this isn't possible, then be as present as (or more present than) the HCP on social media. If an HCP puts out a tweet a day, tweet at least as often. If they post to Facebook three times a day, post relevant information to your site at least three times daily. Keep all your messages brief, clear, calm, factual, and accurate.

And remember, wherever you go, *never* insult the HCP, even indirectly, even in a very private forum, even once. The Wannabe King will find a way to use it against you, calling you abusive and unfair, even as they heap abuse, scorn, and lies on *you*. By not insulting them, you will surprise many people and throw the HCP off balance. This is the secret power of the assertive approach. You will look strong and reasonable, and they won't.

Factual Repetition

Our brains are very susceptible to simple phrases, repeated over and over again, so that we remember them whether we want to or not. That's why advertising jingles work so well.

We have seen that repetition works for Wannabe Kings. High-conflict politicians win votes through emotional repetition of false statements hundreds and thousands of times, until people begin to believe them (or at least take them seriously).

Respond by repeating the same truths hundreds or thousands of times. *Factual repetition* is necessary to get through to people who aren't paying attention or who have an initial positive feeling about the HCP.

If you and an HCP (or their surrogate) appear together in front of an audience, match the high *energy* of the HCP's extreme and emotional statements. But be calm, straightforward, and factual at all times.

Also, you can include emotions in your message. You can be excited or enthusiastic. But avoid high-conflict emotions such as rage, terror, blame, fear, and helplessness.

The ideal message has factual and emotional repetition in it. It also needs to be simple, so that it's memorable.

Keep It Simple

Because of their all-or-nothing thinking, HCPs are highly skilled at promoting simple (and usually utterly false) concepts. They often believe in the simplicity of problems. Heroes and villains says it all for them.

Typically, phrases with three beats in them are the easiest to remember. For example, during the 2016 presidential campaign, Donald Trump had three very common chants at his rallies, each with three beats: "Build the Wall!" "Lock Her Up!" and "Drain the Swamp!" Although these ended up meaning nothing, they became memorized by the entire nation. Our brains like remembering things with three beats, four or five at the most.

Some examples of phrases that oppose an HCP and their fantasy promises might be these:

Trade, not war!

Lots more jobs!

Keep kids safe!

Phrases should include words that produce or suggest positive, mild emotions—*not intensely* strong ones. Strong emotions tend to shut off people's logical thinking. You want thinking *and* emotions to energize people and stimulate their logical memories.

Encourage Everyone to Respond and Repeat

When speaking before a crowd, recognize the presence and energy of that crowd, and use it to promote your (or your candidate's) causes and values. And you can use this opportunity to teach the Fantasy Crisis Triad while you are also bonding with your audience. This is a good time to ask the three key questions from Chapter 5 in a call-and-response manner:

Is _____ really a crisis? [Crowd response:] NO!

Is _____ really a villain? [Crowd response:] NO!

Is _____ really a hero? [Crowd response:] NO!

[If appropriate, you can add]:

Then vote for _____ on _____ ! [Crowd response:] YES!

Such call-and-response interactions connect with people's positive emotions and power without misleading them like Wannabe Kings so often do with their fantasy crisis emotions.

Conclusion

The assertive approach is necessary to confront the endlessly aggressive behavior of HCP Wannabe Kings. Simply put, our society has begun to confuse fantasy and reality. In the ancient past, human beings needed to be adversaries and highly aggressive to survive. In the present, we are too interconnected to be able to afford endlessly aggressive behavior by any individual or group—and especially by our Cultural Leaders.

Our social DNA has allowed us the ability to be both adversarial and cooperative. If we can learn to restrain our leaders and ourselves from too much aggressive behavior and threats of it, we will have a much better chance of long-term survival. It's up to us as citizens of the world *and* as voters.

MANAGE THE MEDIA
AND FAKE NEWS

A free and independent press is essential to democracy and also to limiting the power of high-conflict politicians. In many of the examples in this book, these Wannabe Kings have quickly moved to control and dominate journalists as an essential step toward consolidating their power and eliminating their democracies. Although some Wannabe Kings lock up or kill journalists, others disparage them by calling them "fake news."

This term first arose during the 2016 US presidential election cycle. Because Facebook advertising paid people for the number of clicks they got on their websites, some people in a small town in Macedonia apparently generated fake news stories to draw in huge numbers of users with totally made up headlines such as these: "Pope Francis Shocks World, Endorses Donald Trump for President" and "FBI Agent Suspected in Hillary Email Leaks Found Dead in Apparent Murder-Suicide."[273]

Although these fake stories may have been helping Trump's election prospects, he quickly co-opted the term *fake news* and turned it against the mainstream American news media. His followers then became even more skeptical of news reports critical of Trump, and his opponents predictably became outraged, disenchanted, or mildly confused—and thus Trump succeeded in creating the 4-way voter split.

Trump's approach caught the news media off guard. Without knowing how to respond, they initially simply repeated and repeated all the news that came in—including from these questionable sources—because they were getting wide coverage on the Internet. They repeated everything that Trump said, regardless of its credibility, because first he was a presidential candidate and then the president. Eventually, some news outlets began stating that certain news items were suspect or actually false, and some started digging deeper into the issues rather than simply reporting what the politicians said about each other and what voters said they felt about what the politicians had said.

The media did a great deal of hand-wringing over what they had done wrong or should have done instead. It's understandable that they were confused, because they—along with everyone else in our democracy—thought our nation was a cooperative society. They didn't realize how severely HCPs attack those on the same team.

My conclusion is that media around the world has gotten seduced into focusing on the emotions that are being driven by the Wannabe Kings and their Negative Advocates, rather than focusing on the actual facts. This has certainly been true of the face and voice news media, including radio, television, and social media. Fortunately, print media has driven fact-finding investigations and reporting.

To really deal with the news media and fake news when it seems to be arising, I believe they (the news media) and we should ask the following ten questions:

TEN QUESTIONS FOR FAKE NEWS ANALYSIS

1. Is this really true? Is this really a crisis?

2. What is the context? Is this a representative or exceptional situation?

3. What are the numbers/statistics on this?

4. Do the experts agree? Why or why not?

5. Is this a credible news source?

6. What do other news sources say about this?

7. Is the person or group being blamed really a villain? Are they even connected in any way to this problem?

8. Is the person speaking about the alleged crisis really a hero?

9. Will the speaker personally benefit by saying what they are saying?

10. How likely is it that this is really a projection of what the speaker is saying or doing themselves?

It would be great if these pointed questions and the resulting answers were the kinds of information we received regularly rather than the high-emotion "breaking" news that simply grabs our amygdala to get our attention. But remember, we actually have a choice. We can reinforce the high-emotion news or stop watching it and seek out informational news. It's up to us.

Conclusion

MAINTAINING OUR IMMUNITY

The world will always have high-conflict personalities and high-conflict politicians. They are the greatest threat to humanity if they are not understood and reined in, rather than given more power. The more people who understand their patterns and practice the types of methods described in this book, the safer we will all be.

This isn't a problem we can solve and put behind us any more than we can conquer all disease and dispense with medical care and the human immune system. For as long as there are human beings, roughly 7 to 8 percent of us will be sociopaths or narcissists (or both), and some of these will be HCP Wannabe Kings who are irresistibly drawn to seek unlimited power.

But now you know their patterns. You know that they are preoccupied with attacking endless Targets of Blame. You know that they use Fantasy Crisis Triads to recruit followers. You know that they use emotional warfare to divide their opposition and take down any individual close to them who challenges them or becomes inconvenient. They seduce, attack, divide, and dominate. We must recognize these patterns as early as possible—and we can. And we must remember, this problem is not about the politics; it's about the personalities.

It may appear that Wannabe Kings throughout history have simply taken advantage of extremely deep unique historical resentments to get into power, such as in Hitler's Germany. However, the HCP theory regarding emotional warfare and Fantasy Crisis Triads suggests that HCPs in the last hundred years have used the latest viral media to turn their people into extreme horrific fighting forces against *anyone* they chose to target no matter how absurd. Rather than harnessing a unique history of resentments, it's this power to teach division and splitting in the present that may be the driving force of HCPs. This makes our vigilance and immunity against giving HCPs power even more important everywhere.

All of us, in all countries, in all generations now and to come, need to learn to understand the dynamics of HCPs, and we need to work actively to keep them from gaining power, in the same way that our bodies need to always produce and circulate antibodies.

We can never stop and relax and imagine that the threat of high-conflict politicians is not imminent, and that politics is just about politics, not personalities too. If we do, this is precisely when the next HCP will storm through the gates and seize control. This is probably why so many Wannabe Kings have arisen in the 2000s, when things are generally going better than ever worldwide. We haven't been paying attention and maintaining immunity to the narcissists and sociopaths that have been gaining attention all around us.

But we *can* build awareness and appropriate protections into our culture so that they become as normal as locks on our doors and police on our streets. Only when we have done this can our freedom and democracy—and health and safety—be preserved, year after year. It's up to us—all of us working together—to not allow ourselves to be divided by high-conflict politicians selling fantasy crises, villains, and heroes.

Appendix A

40 PREDICTABLE BEHAVIORS OF HCPs

Excerpted with permission from the book 5 Types of People Who Can Ruin Your Life: Identifying and Dealing with Narcissists, Sociopaths and Other High-Conflict Personalities *by Bill Eddy*

Since high-conflict people (HCPs) tend to treat all of their relationships as inherently adversarial, there are at least 40 things you can generally predict about them, once you see the four primary characteristics of *all-or-nothing thinking, unmanaged emotions, blaming others* and *extreme behaviors*. This is regardless of where they live, their level of intelligence, occupation or social position. They:

1. Won't reflect on their own behavior.
2. Won't have insights about their part in problems.
3. Won't understand why they behave the way they do.
4. Won't change their behavior.
5. Won't seek counseling or any form of real advice.
6. Won't understand why they succeed in the short term (when they are initially charming and persuasive) and why they fail in the long-term (when reality sets in).
7. Will become extremely defensive if someone tells them to change.

8. Will claim their behavior is normal and necessary, given the circumstances.

9. Will lack empathy for others, although they may say the right words.

10. Will be preoccupied with drawing attention to themselves.

11. May be preoccupied with the past; defending their own actions and attacking others.

12. May have a public persona that's very good, covering a negative personality in private.

13. May call others crazy when it's suggested that they are being inappropriate.

14. May bully others, but defend themselves by saying that they were bullied.

15. Will be preoccupied with blaming others, even for very small or non-existent events.

16. Will have lots of energy for blaming others, since they don't spend it on self-reflection.

17. Will have *Targets of Blame,* who are intimate others or people in positions of authority.

18. Will focus on a single Target of Blame and try to control, remove or destroy that person.

19. May assault their Target(s) of Blame financially, reputationally, legally, physically, etc.

20. May engage administrative or legal procedures against their Target(s) of Blame.

21. Will constantly seek *Negative Advocates* to assist in blaming others and defending themselves.

22. Will easily turn against their Negative Advocates when they don't do as they're told.

23. Will demand loyalty from others and tell them what they need to do.

24. Will not be loyal themselves, claiming they were betrayed.

25. May be very secretive, yet demand full disclosure from others, including confidences.

26. May breach confidences about others when it serves their purpose.

27. Will truly wonder why so many people "turn against them" over time.

28. Will turn on family and good friends in an instant; may try to repair the relationship.

29. Will have few, if any, real friends over time.

30. Will not be happy most of the time, except when people totally agree with them.

31. Will have high-intensity relationships, starting with intense attractions but ending with intense resentments and blame.

32. Will have unrealistically high expectations of their allies, which will inevitably be dashed.

33. Will sabotage themselves, working against their own self-interest.

34. Will create many of the problems that they claim they are trying to solve.

35. Will project onto others what they are doing or thinking themselves.

36. Will lack self-restraint, even when it's in their best interests to restrain themselves.

37. Will do things impulsively, then sometimes regret it and other times not regret it.

38. Will ask for many favors, yet will not reciprocate favors.

39. Will respond to requests with unrelated demands, often ignoring the request altogether.

40. Will "split" those around them into all-good and all-bad people, triggering many conflicts.

In general, people are shocked at how intense, but predictable, these behaviors can be. Once they see the four primary characteristics, however, they can focus on avoiding the person or using the methods described in this book to help manage the situation.

Appendix B

HIGH-CONFLICT POLITICIAN SCORECARD

Excerpted with permission from the book Splitting America *by Bill Eddy and Don Saposnek. (High Conflict Institute Press: Scottsdale AZ)*

High-conflict politicians have won elections and then turned into huge mistakes—either getting thrown out of office for their misdeeds or making high-conflict decisions that have cost our nation dearly. In order to help you notice the warning signs, we have come up with a short checklist (on the following page) to consider for potential candidates.

ON-GOING TRAITS:	REGULAR PATTERN OF BEHAVIOR							
	Never	Mild		Moderate		Often		Very Often
Personal Attacks	0	1	2	3	4	5	6	7	8
Crisis Emotions	0	1	2	3	4	5	6	7	8
All-or-nothing solutions	0	1	2	3	4	5	6	7	8
Self-absorbed	0	1	2	3	4	5	6	7	8
Lacks empathy	0	1	2	3	4	5	6	7	8
Misjudges others	0	1	2	3	4	5	6	7	8
Sees self as a big hero	0	1	2	3	4	5	6	7	8
Doesn't play well with others	0	1	2	3	4	5	6	7	8

TOTAL SCORE = _____

This scorecard is proposed as a guide for comparing candidates, and is not a research-based formula. To a great extent, high-conflict behavior is in the eye of the beholder. There is no cut-off or clear line between "reasonable" people and "high-conflict" people. It is possible that some elections are between two candidates who both score high or both score low on this list, while other elections may present more clear-cut situations, with one low and one high. Simply thinking about these behaviors should help you become less vulnerable to attack ads and other manipulations by high-conflict politicians in federal, state and local elections.

Appendix C

BLANK 4-WAY VOTER
SPLIT DIAGRAM

The blank diagram on the next page is provided for you to use in analyzing upcoming elections or looking back on elections. For an example, see Figure 5 in Chapter 8, "US Presidential Election 2016," which includes the players, their roles, and percentages of votes. You can also plug in the percentages from Chapter 6, where you will find the statistics for Hitler's parliamentary election and Stalin's Communist Party election as General Secretary.

4-WAY VOTER SPLIT
Fill-In Your Own

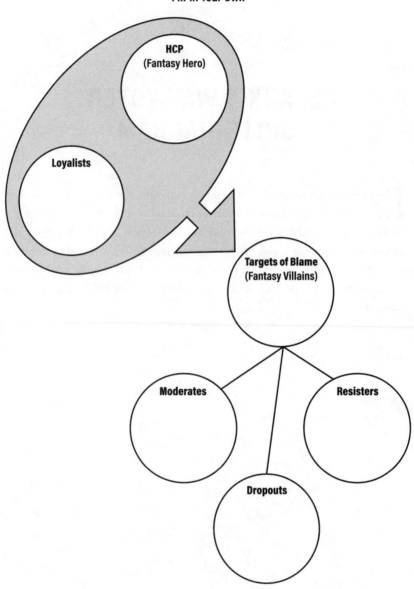

Appendix D

FANTASY CRISIS TRIADS—
EXAMPLES WORLDWIDE

The following charts summarize the Fantasy Crisis Triads of the eleven leaders described in Part II of this book. They are just a small sampling of the many HCP Wannabe Kings over the past one hundred years, who have used modern high-emotion media while damaging or destroying their countries. As you can see, the potential for many more Wannabe Kings has grown over the past thirty years.

FANTASY CRISIS TRIADS: EXAMPLES WORLDWIDE (IN JANUARY 2019)
(Small Sample Worldwide from Part II of this Book)

PLACE AND YEARS	FANTASY CRISIS	FANTASY VILLAIN	FANTASY HERO	HIGH-EMOTION MEDIA	DAMAGE TO PEOPLE AND DEMOCRACY
Germany (1920–1945)	Government "betrayal" lost WWI, Jewish immigrants pouring in	Jews, Communists, Social Democrats	Hitler	Controlled media; constantly talked on the radio to everyone in their homes in Germany	Caused deaths of over fifty-five million people by starting WWII
Russia (1917–1952)	Tsarist government, famines, resistance to collectivization	Tsar, Kulaks, counter-revolutionaries, the West, spies, everyone	Stalin	Totally controlled media; gave constant speeches	Caused deaths of over twenty million people
China (1935–1976)	Chinese government and landowners, resistance to collectivization	Chinese nationalists, peasant farmers opposed to collectivization, urban elite	Mao	Totally controlled media, posted airbrushed photo of himself everywhere; projected voice everywhere on public speakers	Caused deaths of about forty million people (primarily from famines he caused)
Russia (2000–Present)	Propaganda of Homosexuality, Western culture, American politicians	Political enemies were pedophiles working throughout government, homosexuals, Hillary Clinton, George Soros, and U.S. Ambassador Michael McFaul	Putin	Controlled media after first year in office; pushed media owners out; gave constant speeches about fantasy crises	Continues to cause an unknown number of deaths, imprisonments, and disappearances of opponents; presides over undemocratic elections; appoints governors and many legislators

Continues

Continued

FANTASY CRISIS TRIADS: EXAMPLES WORLDWIDE (IN JANUARY 2019)
(Small Sample Worldwide from Part II of this Book)

PLACE AND YEARS	FANTASY CRISIS	FANTASY VILLAIN	FANTASY HERO	HIGH-EMOTION MEDIA	DAMAGE TO PEOPLE AND DEMOCRACY
Hungary (2010–Present)	European Union, immigration, treated as victims by West, attack on traditional family values	Muslim immigrants; George Soros; European Union and Western officials	Orban	Curbed the media; controls media regulators, visually manipulates news	Controls selection of judiciary (all now have been appointed by Orban's people), has redrawn election maps to favor his party
Venezuela (2013–Present)	Wealthy landowners and business people, Enemies of the people's revolution	Oil companies, wealthy Venezuelans, counter-revolutionaries, United States, Donald Trump	Maduro	Closed major TV station, constantly gives long speeches	Replaced democratically elected legislature with his own "constituent assembly"
Italy (1994–Present)	Taxes being heavily increased by Communists and liberals; privileges being taken away	Communists, liberals	Berlusconi	Owned three TV stations, constantly self-promoted "I am the Jesus Christ of politics," owned 90 percent of TV audience and advertising	Did nothing to improve lives as he promised; created conditions for newly destabilized, less democratic government
US (1950–1954)	Communists want to take over the United States from the inside	Communists working throughout federal government and army	McCarthy	Televised nationwide aggressively interrogating people he suspected	Ruined lives and reputations; blacklisted people couldn't get work; instilled widespread fear of neighbors, co-workers, etc.

Continues

Continued

FANTASY CRISIS TRIADS: EXAMPLES WORLDWIDE (IN JANUARY 2019)
(Small Sample Worldwide from Part II of this Book)

PLACE AND YEARS	FANTASY CRISIS	FANTASY VILLAIN	FANTASY HERO	HIGH-EMOTION MEDIA	DAMAGE TO PEOPLE AND DEMOCRACY
US (1968–1974)	Chaos, law and order, Communists, protesters of War in Vietnam, "mob rule"	Minorities and students protesting, Communists in Vietnam and Cambodia; journalists, enemies list	Nixon	Used speeches on TV and radio without allowing commentary response; drummed up fear of minorities, protesters, "mob rule"	Was behind break-in of Democratic presidential campaign headquarters; threatened media and "enemies" with the use of Federal agencies against them (IRS, FCC, DOJ, etc.)
US (2016–present)	Mexican immigrants "pouring in," Muslims, journalists, Obamacare	Former President Obama, Hillary Clinton, Mexicans, Muslims, African-Americans, China, Canada, European Union, NATO allies	Trump	Uses Twitter daily; holds frequent rallies; gives frequent TV interviews; uses Fox News to serve as his own media	Efforts to intimidate and block press from events; inspired increase in hate crimes against minorities; efforts toward one-party government, including judiciary
_____ ? Next unknown country (there are several others already since 2000)	Nonexistent problems presented as "crises." Real problems presented as "crises" requiring a hero	Individuals who look different, small groups of people (1–3 percent of population), government "establishment," media and individual journalists	? _____ Next Wannabe King	Constant inflammatory speeches and use of fake news on social media, Fantasy Crisis Triads	Authoritarian rule

NOTES

1. Steven Pinker, *The Better Angels of Our Nature: Why Violence Has Declined* (New York: Viking, 2011), 520.
2. Pinker, *Better Angels*, 195.
3. William Shirer, *The Rise and Fall of the Third Reich* (New York: Rosetta Books LLC, 2011), loc. 31–32 of 4175, iBooks.
4. Pinker, *Better Angels*, 208.
5. Anne Applebaum, *Red Famine: Stalin's War on Ukraine* (New York: Doubleday, 2017), 280.
6. Applebaum, *Red Famine*, 186.
7. Applebaum, 120.
8. Pinker, *Better Angels*, 331.
9. Pinker, 343.
10. Pinker, 524–525.
11. BBC News, "Serbia Captures Fugitive Karadzic," July 22, 2008, http://news.bbc .co.uk/2/hi/europe/7518543.stm.
12. Andrew Nagorski, *Hitlerland: American Eyewitnesses to the Nazi Rise to Power* (New York: Simon and Schuster Paperbacks, 2012), 148.
13. Nagorski, 324.
14. American Psychiatric Association, *Diagnostic and Statistical Manual of Mental Disorders, Fifth Edition: DSM-5* (Arlington, VA: American Psychiatric Association, 2013), 646. (Hereafter "APA, DSM-5.")
15. Jean Twenge and W. Keith Campbell, *The Narcissism Epidemic: Living in the Age of Entitlement* (New York: Free Press, 2009).
16. APA, DSM-5, 659 and 669–670.
17. APA, DSM-5, 646.
18. APA, DSM-5, 669–670.
19. Twenge, *Narcissism Epidemic*, 45.
20. Frederick Stinson et al., "Prevalence, Correlates, Disability, and Comorbidity of DSM-IV Narcissistic Personality Disorder: Results from the Wave 2 National Epidemiologic Survey on Alcohol and Related Conditions," *Journal of Clinical Psychiatry* 69, no. 7 (July 2008):1033–45, 1036.

21. APA, DSM-5, 659.

22. Bridget Grant et al., "Prevalence, Correlates, and Disability of Personality Disorders in the United States: Results from the National Epidemiologic Survey on Alcohol and Related Conditions," *Journal of Clinical Psychiatry* 65, no. 7 (July 2004): 948–58, 952.

23. Paul Babiak and Robert Hare, *Snakes in Suits: When Psychopaths Go to Work* (Toronto: HarperCollins Publishers, 2006).

24. APA, DSM-5, 662.

25. Otto Kernberg, MD, an expert on diagnosing and treating narcissists and sociopaths, stated this in a presentation at the Evolution of Psychotherapy Conference, Anaheim, CA, December 16, 2017, attended by the author.

26. John Gartner, "DEFCON 2: Nuclear Risk Is Rising as Donald Trump Goes Downhill," in *Rocket Man: Nuclear Madness and the Mind of Donald Trump*, ed. John Gartner, Steven Buser, and Leonard Cruz (Asheville, NC: Chiron Publications, 2018), 29.

27. Erich Fromm, *The Heart of Man: It's Genius for Good and Evil* (Riverdale, NY: American Mental Health Foundation; First published by Harper and Row, Publishers, New York, 1964), loc. 998 of 2243, Kindle.

28. Fromm, *Heart of Man*, loc. 998 of 2243.

29. Stinson et al., "Prevalence . . . Narcissistic Personality," 1038.

30. *United States v. Mitchell* (2010) 706 F. Supp. 2d 1148.

31. *Guilbeau v. Guilbeau* (1996) 85F 3d 1149, 1154.

32. Pinker, *Better Angels*, 329.

33. Pinker, 330.

34. Nagorski, *Hitlerland*, 35.

35. Applebaum, *Red Famine*, 116.

36. Applebaum, 116.

37. Nagorski, *Hitlerland*, 299.

38. Theodore Millon, *Disorders of Personality: DSM-IV and Beyond* (New York: John Wiley and Sons, 1996), 84.

39. Joseph Burgo, *The Narcissist You Know: Defending Yourself Against Extreme Narcissists in an All-About-Me Age* (New York: Touchstone, 2015).

40. Shirer, *Third Reich*, loc. 87–88 of 4174, iBooks.

41. Applebaum, *Red Famine*, 83–84.

42. Nagorski, *Hitlerland*, 76.

43. Nagorski, 95.

44. Applebaum, *Red Famine*, 90.

45. Applebaum, 7.

46. Applebaum, 35.

47. Applebaum, 37.

48. Applebaum, 126.

49. Applebaum, 280.

50. Daniel Goleman, *Social Intelligence: The New Science of Human Relationships* (New York: A Bantam Book, 2006), 40.

51. Goleman, *Social Intelligence*, 43.

52. Goleman, 48.

53. Applebaum, *Red Famine*, 231.

54. John Hibbing, Kevin Smith, and John Alford, *Predisposed: Liberals, Conservatives, and the Biology of Political Differences* (New York: Routledge, 2014), loc. 635 of 1039, iBooks.

55. Robert Sapolski, *Behave: The Biology of Humans at Our Best and Worst* (New York: Penguin Press, 2017), 450-–451.

56. Sapolski, *Behave*, 452.

57. Sapolski, 451.

58. Sapolski, 452.

59. Hibbing, *Predisposed*, loc. 869 of 1039.

60. David Brooks, *The Social Animal: The Hidden Sources of Love, Character, and Achievement* (New York: Random House, 2011), 302–303.

61. John Bargh, "At Yale, We Conducted an Experiment to Turn Conservatives into Liberals. The Results Say a Lot about Our Political Divisions," *Washington Post*, November 22, 2017.

62. Sapolsky, *Behave*, 453.

63. Bargh, *At Yale*.

64. Masha Gessen, *The Future Is History: How Totalitarianism Reclaimed Russia* (New York: Riverhead Books, 2017), loc. 864 of 1507, iBooks.

65. Bob Woodward, *Fear: Trump in the White House* (New York: Simon and Schuster, 2018).

66. Farhad Manjoo, "We Have Reached Peak Screen. Now Revolution Is in the Air," *New York Times*, June 27, 2018, https://www.nytimes.com/2018/06/27/technology/peak-screen-revolution.html.

67. Soroush Vosoughi, Deb Roy, and Sinan Aral, "The Spread of True and False News Online," *Science*, May 9, 2018, 1146–1141, http://science.sciencemag.org/content/359/6380/1146.

68. Michelle Goldberg, "Democrats Should Un-friend Facebook," *New York Times*, November 16, 2018, https://www.nytimes.com/2018/11/16/opinion/facebook-mark-zuckerberg-sheryl-sandberg-silicon-valley-antitrust.html.

69. The Editorial Board, "The War on Truth Spreads," *New York Times*, December 9, 2018, https://www.nytimes.com/2018/12/09/opinion/media-duterte-maria-ressa.html.

70. Marshall McLuhan, *The Medium Is the Massage: An Inventory of Effects* (New York: Penguin Books, 1964).

71. Manjoo, "Peak Screen."

72. Steven Pinker, *Enlightenment Now: The Case for Reason, Science, Humanism, and Progress* (New York: Viking, An imprint of Penguin Random House LLC, 2018).

73. Pinker, *Enlightenment*, 42.

74. Pinker, 50.

75. McKay Coppins, "The Man Who Broke Politics," *Atlantic*, October 17, 2018, https://www.theatlantic.com/magazine/archive/2018/11/newt-gingrich -says-youre-welcome/570832/.

76. Coppins, "The Man."

77. Brooks Boliek, "FCC Finally Kills Off Fairness Doctrine," *Politico*, August 22, 2018, https://www.politico.com/story/2011/08/fcc-finally-kills-off-fairness -doctrine-061851.

78. Gabriel Sherman, *The Loudest Voice in the Room: How the Brilliant, Bombastic Roger Ailes Built Fox News—And Divided a Country* (New York: Random House, 2014, 2017).

79. Sherman, *Loudest Voice*, 699–702 of 1763, iBooks.

80. Sherman, 27. (All of these page numbers for Sherman are "of 1763.")

81. Sherman, 978.

82. Sherman, 28.

83. Sherman, 26.

84. Pinker, *Enlightenment*, 51.

85. Pinker, 52.

86. Benjamin Franklin, "One Of The Central Documents In The History Of Western Civilization . . . The Symbol Of Political Liberty": *The Magna Carta*, Boston, 1721, Printed By The Firm Of 15-Year-Old Apprentice Benjamin Franklin.

87. Nagorski, *Hitlerland*, 99–100.

88. Abigail Tracy, "George W. Bush Finally Says What He Thinks about Trump. He Didn't Even Have to Say the President's Name." *Vanity Fair*, October 19, 2017, https://www.vanityfair.com/news/2017/10/george-w-bush-donald-trump.

89. Shirer, *Third Reich*, 63 of 4174.

90. Shirer, 56. (All of these page numbers for Shirer are "of 4174")

91. Shirer, 56–58.

92. Shirer, 78–79.

93. Shirer, 103–104.

94. Peter Ross Range, *1924: The Year That Made Hitler* (New York: Little, Brown and Company, 2016), 52 of 817, iBooks.

95. Range, 1924, 36 of 817.

96. Shirer, *Third Reich*, 121 of 4175.

97. Shirer, 233 of 4174.

98. United States Holocaust Memorial Museum, "Germany: Jewish Population in 1933, *Holocaust Encyclopedia,* retrieved on November 3, 2018. https:// encyclopedia.ushmm.org/content/en/article/germany-jewish-population -in-1933.

99. Daniel Jonah Goldhagen, *Hitler's Willing Executioners: Ordinary Germans and the Holocaust* (New York: Random House, 1996, 1997).

100. Nagorski, *Hitlerland,* 85.

101. Nagorski, 68–69.

102. Nagorski, 84.

103. Nagorski, 95.

104. Nagorski, 105.

105. Nagorski, 163.

106. Nagorski, 101.

107. Orlando Figes, "From Tsar to U.S.S.R.: Russian's Chaotic Year of Revolution," *National Geographic History Magazine,* Oct. 25, 2017, https://www .nationalgeographic.com/archaeology-and-history/magazine/2017/09-10 /russian-revolution-history-lenin/.

108. Simon Sebag Montefiore, *Young Stalin* (New York: Vintage Books, a Division of Random House, Inc., 2007), 23.

109. Montefiore, *Young Stalin,* 29.

110. Montefiore, 28.

111. Montefiore, 34.

112. Montefiore, 32.

113. Montefiore, 37.

114. Montefiore, 38.

115. Keith Gessen, "How Stalin Became Stalinist," *New Yorker,* November 6, 2017, https://www.newyorker.com/magazine/2017/11/06/how-stalin-became -stalinist.

116. Stephen Kotkin, *Stalin: Paradoxes of Power, 1878–1928* (New York: Penguin Books, 2014), loc. 411–412 of 740, Kindle.

117. K. Gessen, "How Stalin."

118. Montefiore, 42.

119. Montefiore, 42.

120. Appelbaum, *Red Famine,* 82.

121. K. Gessen, "How Stalin."

122. K. Gessen, "How Stalin."

123. Nagorski, *Hitlerland,* 299.

124. Pinker, *Better Angels,* 195.

125. Wikipedia, "Republic of China (1912-1949)," retrieved on 12/17/18 from https://en.wikipedia.org/wiki/Republic_of_China_(1912%E2%80%931949).

126. Jung Chang and Jon Halliday, *Mao: The Unknown Story* (New York: Anchor Books, a division of Random House, 2005, 2006), loc. 69 of 4089, iBooks.

127. Chang, *Mao*, loc. 74 of 4089.

128. Chang, 132. (All of these page numbers for Chang are "of 4089.")

129. Chang, 102–03.

130. Chang, 106–08.

131. Chang, 134–35.

132. Chang, 710.

133. Chang, 708.

134. Chang, 718–20.

135. Chang, 768.

136. Chang, 747.

137. Chang, 521–22.

138. Pinker, *Better Angels*, 332.

139. Pinker, 322.

140. Chang, *Mao*, 2477–2478.

141. Chang, 2479.

142. I personally saw his tomb and photo when I was in Tiananmen Square in Beijing China in 2014.

143. Steven Lee Myers, *The New Tsar: The Rise and Reign of Vladimir Putin* (New York: A Borzoi Book, Published by Alfred A. Knopf, a division of Penguin Random House, Ltd., 2015), 15.

144. Myers, *New Tsar*, 15.

145. Myers, 16.

146. Myers, 17.

147. M. Gessen, *Future Is History*, 588–589 of 1507.

148. M. Gessen, 588–89.

149. M. Gessen, 202.

150. McFaul, *From Cold War to Hot Peace: An American Ambassador in Putin's Russia* (New York: Houghton Mifflin Harcourt Publishing Company, 2018), 886 of 1928.

151. M. Gessen, *Future Is History*, 593.

152. M. Gessen, 639–40.

153. M. Gessen, 642.

154. McFaul, *Cold War*, loc. 845–847 of 1928.

155. McFaul, 887.

156. McFaul, 894.

157. McFaul, 230–31.

158. Misha Friedman, "Babushkas for Putin," *New York Times*, March 15, 2018, https://www.nytimes.com/2018/03/15/opinion/sunday/babushkas-for-putin.html.

159. McFaul, 223–24.

160. Neil Buckley and Andrew Byrne, "The Rise and Rise of Viktor Orban," *Financial Times*, January 24, 2018, https://www.ft.com/content/dda50a3e-0095 -11e8-9650-9c0ad2d7c5b5.

161. Patrick Kingsley, "As West Fears the Rise of Autocrats, Hungary Shows What's Possible," *New York Times*, February 10, 2018, https://www.nytimes .com/2018/02/10/world/europe/hungary-orban-democracy-far-right.html.

162. Kingsley, "As the West."

163. Michael Steinberger, "George Soros Bet Big on Liberal Democracy. Now He Fears He Is Losing," *New York Times*, July 18, 2018, https://www.nytimes .com/2018/07/17/magazine/george-soros-democrat-open-society.html.

164. New York Times Board, "Viktor Orban's Perversion of Democracy in Hungary," *New York Times*, April 5, 2018, https://www.nytimes.com/2018/04/05 /opinion/viktor-orban-hungary-election.html.

165. Kingsley, "As the West."

166. Marc Santora, "Hungary Election Gives Orban Big Majority, and Control of Constitution," *New York Times*, April 8, 2018, https://www.nytimes .com/2018/04/08/world/europe/hungary-election-viktor-orban.html.

167. Santora, "Hungary Election."

168. Floyd Whaley, "30 Years After Revolution, Some Filipinos Yearn for 'Golden Age' of Marcos," *New York Times*, February 23, 2016, https://www.nytimes .com/2016/02/24/world/asia/30-years-after-revolution-some-filipinos-yearn -for-golden-age-of-marcos.html.

169. "Rodrigo Duterte Biography," thefamouspeople.com, retrieved on December 20, 2018, from https://www.thefamouspeople.com/profiles/rodrigo- duterte-7713.php.

170. "Rodrigo Duterte Biography."

171. Christopher Caldwell, "The Killa in Manila," *Weekly Standard*, August 11, 2018, https://www.weeklystandard.com/christopher-caldwell/understanding -the-popularity-of-philippines-president-rodrigo-duterte.

172. Caldwell, "The Killa."

173. Caldwell, "The Killa."

174. Caldwell, "The Killa."

175. Caldwell, "The Killa."

176. Caldwell, "The Killa."

177. Caldwell, "The Killa."

178. Caldwell, "The Killa."

179. Jon Lee Anderson, "Nicolas Maduro's Accelerating Revolution," *New Yorker*, December 11, 2017, https://www.newyorker.com/search/q/Accelerating %20Revolution.

180. Anderson, "Maduro's Revolution."

181. Eduardo Sanchez, "Maduro—Traits of a Paranoid Personality," Center for Conflict Studies: Leader Profiles, January 13, 2014, http://sites.miis.edu/ccsprofilesofworldleaders/2014/01/13/maduro-traits-of-a-paranoid-personality/.

182. Associated Press, "Venezuela's Maduro: US Leads Assassination Plot against Him," *New York Times*, December 12, 2018, https://www.nytimes.com/aponline/2018/12/12/world/americas/ap-lt-venezuela-maduro.html.

183. Anderson, "Maduro's Revolution."

184. Associated Press, "Maduro's Grip on Venezuela Tightens, Warns of Trump Threat," *New York Times*, December 9, 2018, https://www.nytimes.com/aponline/2018/12/09/world/americas/ap-lt-venezuela-local-elections.html.

185. Anderson, "Maduro's Revolution."

186. Anderson, "Maduro's Revolution."

187. Alan Friedman, *Berlusconi: The Epic Story of the Billionaire Who Took Over Italy* (New York: Hachette Books, 2015), loc. 31–33 of 703, iBooks.

188. Alan Friedman, *Berlusconi*, 50 of 703.

189. Friedman, 42–50. (All of these page numbers for Friedman are "of 703".)

190. Friedman, 17.

191. The Local, "'Berlusconi Has a Personality Disorder,'" thelocal.it, November 27, 2013, https://www.thelocal.it/20131127/berlusconi-has-a-personality-disorder.

192. Friedman, 201–235.

193. Friedman, 548.

194. Michael Hirst, "Berlusconi Says He Is Like Jesus," *Telegraph*, February 13, 2006, https://www.telegraph.co.uk/news/worldnews/europe/italy/1510375/Berlusconi-says-he-is-like-Jesus.html.

195. Friedman, 386.

196. Darien Pavli, "Berlusconi's Chilling Effect on Italian Media," Open Society Foundations, March 30, 2010, https://www.opensocietyfoundations.org/voices/berlusconi-s-chilling-effect-italian-media.

197. Steven Levitsky and Daniel Ziblatt, *How Democracies Die* (New York: Crown Publishing Group, a division of Penguin Random House, 2018), 105.

198. Levitsky and Ziblatt, *How Democracies*, 99–104.

199. Jeff Guin, *The Road to Jonestown: Jim Jones and Peoples Temple* (New York: Simon and Schuster, 2017).

200. "Joseph McCarthy Biography," *Encyclopedia of World Biography*, December 24, 2018, https://www.notablebiographies.com/Ma-Mo/McCarthy-Joseph.html.

201. Editors, "McCarthy Says Communists Are in State Department," History.com, December 13, 2018, https://www.history.com/this-day-in-history/mccarthy-says-communists-are-in-state-department.

202. Stanley Karnow, *Vietnam: A History* (New York: Penguin Group, 1983, 1991, 1997), 593.

203. Levitsky and Ziblatt, *How Democracies*, 140.

204. Levitsky and Ziblatt, 141.

205. Levitsky and Ziblatt, 102–03.

206. Vamik Volkan, Norman Itzkowitz, and Andrew Dod, *Richard Nixon: A Psychobiography* (New York: Columbia University Press, 1997), 32–35.

207. Volkan, *Richard Nixon*, 91.

208. Volkan, 95.

209. Patrick Buchanan, *The Greatest Comeback: How Richard Nixon Rose from Defeat to Create the New Majority* (New York: Crown Forum, an imprint of Crown Publishing Group, a division of Random House LLC, 2014), 119.

210. Robert Dallek, *Nixon and Kissinger: Partners in Power* (New York: HarperCollins Publishers, 2007), 66.

211. Volkan, *Richard Nixon*, 129.

212. Oscar Winberg, "When It Comes to Harassing the Media, Trump Is No Nixon," *Washington Post*, October 16, 2017, https://www.washingtonpost.com/news/made-by-history/wp/2017/10/16/when-it-comes-to-harassing-the-media-trump-is-no-nixon/?utm_term=.aa2323ceaf86.

213. Winberg, "Trump Is No Nixon."

214. Paul Schwartzman and Michael Miller, "Confident. Incorrigible. Bully: Little Donny Was a Lot Like Candidate Donald Trump," *Washington Post*, June 22, 2016, https://www.washingtonpost.com/lifestyle/style/young-donald-trump-military-school/2016/06/22/f0b3b164-317c-11e6-8758-d58e76e11b12_story.html?utm_term=.a28c307bb9e3.

215. Joseph Burgo, *The Narcissist You Know: Defending Yourself against Extreme Narcissists in an All-About-Me Age* (New York: Touchstone, an imprint of Simon and Schuster, 2015), loc. 502 of 757, iBooks.

216. Burgo, *The Narcissist*, loc. 510–511 of 757.

217. Woodward, *Fear*, loc. 27 of 210.

218. Julia Glum, "Some Republicans Still Think Obama Was Born in Kenya as Trump Resurrects Birther Conspiracy Theory," *Newsweek*, December 11, 2017, https://www.newsweek.com/trump-birther-obama-poll-republicans-kenya-744195.

219. John Sides, Michael Tesler and Lynn Vavreck, *Identity Crisis: The 2016 Presidential Campaign and the Battle for the Meaning of America* (Princeton: Princeton University Press, 2018), loc. 1864 of 9466, Kindle.

220. David Brooks, "A Little Reality on Immigration," *New York Times*, February 19, 2016, https://www.nytimes.com/2016/02/19/opinion/a-little-reality-on-immigration.html.

221. *Time* Staff, "Here's Donald Trump's Presidential Announcement Speech," *Time,* June 16, 2015, http://time.com/3923128/donald-trump-announcement -speech/.

222. *Time,* "Here's Donald."

223. Yoni Appelbaum, "'I Alone Can Fix It,'" *Atlantic,* July 21, 2016, https://www .theatlantic.com/politics/archive/2016/07/trump-rnc-speech-alone-fix-it /492557/.

224. *Time,* "Here's Donald."

225. "Kaiser Health Tracking Poll: The Public's Views on the ACA," Kaiser Family Foundation, November 28, 2018, https://www.kff.org/interactive/kaiser -health-tracking-poll-the-publics-views-on-the-aca/#?response= Favorable--Unfavorable&aRange=twoYear.

226. Jenna Johnson, "Trump's Grand Promises to 'Very, Very Quickly' Repeal Obamacare Run into Reality," *Washington Post,* July 18, 2017, https://www .washingtonpost.com/politics/trumps-grand-promises-to-very-very-quickly -repeal-obamacare-run-into-reality/2017/07/18/91b5f220-6bd3-11e7-9c15 -177740635e83_story.html?noredirect=on&utm_term=.acdfc3b7221f.

227. Louis Jacobson, "Trump Says U.S. Pulling Out of Paris Climate Agreement," *Politifact,* June 1, 2017, https://www.politifact.com/truth-o-meter/promises /trumpometer/promise/1379/cancel-paris-climate-agreement/.

228. Woodward, *Fear,* 1037 of 1354.

229. Glenn Thrush, "Trump Claims Nafta Victory but Deal Faces Long Odds in U.S.," *New York Times,* November 30, 2018, https://www.nytimes.com/2018 /11/30/us/trump-nafta-usmca-signing.html.

230. Stanley B. Greenberg, "Trump Is Beginning to Lose His Grip," *New York Times,* Nov. 17, 2018, https://www.nytimes.com/2018/11/17/opinion/sunday/trump -is-beginning-to-lose-his-grip.html.

231. David Wasserman, "2016 National Popular Vote Tracker, Cook Report." Retrieved on 12/15/18 from https://docs.google.com/spreadsheets/d /133Eb4qQmOxNvtesw2hdVns073R68EZx4SfCnP4IGQf8/htmlview?sle =true#gid=19.

232. "Voting and Registration in the Election of 2016," United States Census Bureau, May 2017, https://www.census.gov/data/tables/time-series/demo /voting-and-registration/p20-580.html.

233. Sides, *Identity Crisis,* 1844 of 9466. (All of these page numbers for Sides are "of 9466.")

234. Sides, 3226.

235. Sides, 3417.

236. Samara Klar and Yanna Krupnikov, "How to Win Swing Voters (and How to Lose Them)," *New York Times,* October 17, 2018, https://www.nytimes.com /2018/10/17/opinion/midterms-independents-swing-voters-.html.

237. Samara Klar and Yanna Krupnikov, *Independent Politics: How American Disdain for Parties Leads to Political Inaction* (New York: Cambridge University Press, 2016), 7.

238. Klar and Krupnikov, "Swing Voters."

239. Sides, *Identity Crisis*, 2401.

240. Sides, 3394.

241. David Leonhardt, "Voter Suppression Is No Excuse," *New York Times*, October 9, 2018, https://www.nytimes.com/2018/10/09/opinion/voter-suppression-minorities-republican-party-.html?rref=collection%2Fsectioncollection%2Fopinion-columnists.

242. Michael D. Shear and Thomas Gibbons-Neff, "Trump Sending 5,200 Troops to the Border in an Election-Season Response to Migrants," *New York Times*, October 29, 2018, https://www.nytimes.com/2018/10/29/us/politics/border-security-troops-trump.html?module=inline.

243. Shear, "Trump Sending."

244. Maggie Haberman and Mark Landler, "A Week After the Midterms, Trump Seems to Forget the Caravan," *New York Times*, Nov. 7, 2018, https://www.nytimes.com/2018/11/13/us/politics/trump-caravan-midterms.html.

245. Greenberg, "Trump Is Beginning."

246. Charles Bethea, "Word of the Day: Stumped," *New Yorker*, April 11, 2016, https://www.newyorker.com/magazine/2016/04/11/examining-the-vocabulary-of-the-presidential-race.

247. Shawn Musgrave and Matthew Nussbaum, "Trump Thrives in Areas That Lack Traditional News Outlets," April 8, 2018, https://www.politico.com/story/2018/04/08/news-subscriptions-decline-donald-trump-voters-505605.

248. Ross Douthat, "Trump Hacked the Media Right Before Our Eyes," *New York Times*, March 21, 2018, https://www.nytimes.com/2018/03/21/opinion/trump-facebook-cambridge-analytica-media.html.

249. Sides, *Identity Crisis*, 374.

250. Sides, 4633.

251. Sides, 3727.

252. Sides, 1210.

253. Eric Levitz, "Here's Why Trump's Approval Rating Has Gone Up," *New York Magazine*, May 16, 2018, http://nymag.com/daily/intelligencer/2018/05/heres-why-president-trumps-approval-rating-has-gone-up.html.

254. Kareem Fahim, "Erdogan Capitalizes on Trump's Effort to Break and Isolate Turkey," *Washington Post*, August 19, 2018, https://www.washingtonpost.com/world/erdogan-capitalizes-on-trumps-effort-to-break-and-isolate-turkey/2018/08/19/3f6154ba-a17e-11e8-a3dd-2a1991f075d5_story.html?utm_term=.ca03307cb8f2.

255. Nagorski, *Hitlerland*, 3–4.

256. Nagorski, 92.

257. Jens Manuel Krogstad and Mark Hugo Lopez, "Black Voter Turnout Fell in 2016, Even as a Record Number of Americans Cast Ballots," Pew Research, May 12, 2017, http://www.pewresearch.org/fact-tank/2017/05/12/black-voter -turnout-fell-in-2016-even-as-a-record-number-of-americans-cast-ballots/.

258. Nagorski, *Hitlerland*, 69.

259. Pinker, *Better Angels*, 521.

260. Ronald Reagan, *An American Life* (New York: Simon and Schuster, 1990), 150.

261. Michelle Obama, *Becoming Michelle Obama* (Crown Publishing Group, a division of Penguin Random House LLC, 2018), 407.

262. Shirer, *Rise*, 87–88 of 4174.

263. Krogstad and Lopez, "Black Voter."

264. Lauren Gambino, "John McCain: 10 Moments That Will Shape the Senator's Legacy," *Guardian*, August 25, 2018, https://www.theguadian.com/us-news /2018/aug/25/john-mccain-death-moments-life-shape-legacy.

265. Tracey Jan, "They Said I Was Going to Work Like a Donkey. I Was So Grateful," *Washington Post*, July 11, 2017, https://www.washingtonpost.com/news /wonk/wp/2017/07/11/they-said-i-was-going-to-work-like-a-donkey-i-was -grateful/?utm_term=.90be41d949fd.

266. Anna Flagg, "The Myth of the Criminal Immigrant," *New York Times*, March 30, 2018, https://www.nytimes.com/interactive/2018/03/30/upshot/crime -immigration-myth.html.

267. Michael Barbarro, "Once Impervious, Marco Rubio Is Diminished by a Caustic Chris Christie, *New York Times*, February 7, 2016, https://www.nytimes .com/2016/02/07/us/politics/chris-christie-marco-rubio-gop-debate.html.

268. Cass R. Sunstein and Reid Hastie, *Wiser: Getting Beyond Groupthink to Make Groups Smarter* (Boston: Harvard Business Review Press, 2015), 86.

269. Sherman, *Loudest Voice*, 324.

270. Jeremy Heimans and Henry Timms, *New Power: How Power Works in Our Hyperconnected World—And How to Make It Work for You* (New York: Doubleday, a division of Penguin Random House, 2018), 11 of 325, Kindle.

271. Heimans and Timms, *New Power*, 168 of 325.

272. Nicholas Kristoff, "A War Hero or a Phony?" *New York Times*, September 18, 2004, https://www.nytimes.com/2004/09/18/opinion/a-war-hero-or-a-phony .html.

273. Mike Wendling, "The (Almost) Complete History of 'Fake News.'" *BBC Trending*, January 22, 2018, https://www.bbc.com/news/blogs-trending-42724320.

ACKNOWLEDGMENTS

This book is the product of many discussions with many people over many years. I am especially indebted to my wife, Alice, who has encouraged my writing, challenged my thinking, tolerated my intense preoccupation with this book, and generously shared her low-conflict lifestyle with me for over three decades.

I owe a special thanks to my agent, Scott Edelstein, and his wife, Ariella Tilsen. She gets credit for coming up with the premise of this book after a discussion they had about the world situation. Scott gets credit for creating the title and insisting that I was the person who should write this book—and do it quickly.

I would like to thank Megan Hunter, who cofounded the High Conflict Institute with me over ten years ago, as well as the speakers and staff who regularly sharpen my thinking about understanding and managing high-conflict situations and personalities.

I honor the memory of my parents, Margaret and Roland Eddy, and my stepmother, Helen Eddy, who gave me an open-minded upbringing, a sense of service, empathy for others, and excitement about always learning.

The following family and friends gave me very specific and helpful feedback: Cathy Eddy, Alice Fichandler, Dennis Doyle, and Norma Mark. I also appreciate my friends LaRue and Phil Rockhold for providing a wonderful cabin in the woods for writing some key parts of this book, and Bonnie Elias and Stewart Kocivar for adding to the inspiration and discussions.

Last, but not least, I want to thank the team at Berrett-Koehler Publishers—and it really is a team. The key diagram of this book in Chapter 3 (4-Way Voter Split) clicked into place in my mind—and on their whiteboard—when they had me present my book concepts to the entire office. I especially appreciate my editor Anna Leinberger for overall guidance; my copyeditor Rebecca Rider for her very detailed and accurate changes and additions (and tolerance of my occasional resistance); and Jeevan Sivasubramaniam for his always-encouraging editorial supervision. I appreciate the early feedback from these reviewers of my first draft: Mark Annett, Jill Swenson, Jessa Orluk, Deborah Nikkel, and Sarah Modlin. I thank Lasell Whipple and Maureen Forys for their creative (and fun) design, Michael Crowley and Katie Sheehan for their wise marketing advice (and helping me overcome my marketing hesitations), and Chloe Wong and Shabnam Banerjee-McFarland for their work on the endorsements of the book. And finally, I am excited to work again with Kelli Daniels as the publicist in making this another widely read book on this difficult topic of high-conflict personalities.

INDEX

villains and heroes, 105–106,
119–120
warning signs, 118
Tsar Nicholas II, 66–67
Turkey, Recep Tayyip Erdogan, 84, 121

U

United States
Constitution, 46
Fantasy Crisis Triad, 179–180
uniting groups, 128

V

Venezuela
Fantasy Crisis Triad, 179
Nicolas Maduro, 88–91
Vietnam War, 100–101
villains and heroes
avoiding emotional attacks,
150–152
avoiding emotional defense,
152–153
Berlusconi, Silvio, 92–93
cultural leadership, 45–46
Duterte, Rodrigo, 86–87
fantasizing, 45–47, 50–55, 57,
150–153, 174
Fantasy Crisis Triad, 50–51, 54–55
Hitler, Adolf, 64–66
Maduro, Nicolas, 89–90
Mao Zedong, 74–75
McCarthy, Joseph, 97–98
mistake of believing in, 119–120
Nixon, Richard, 101
Orban, Viktor, 83–84

political leadership, 47
Putin, Vladimir, 79–80
responding to, 150–153
Stalin, Josef, 70
three key questions, 57
Trump, Donald, 105–106
"voter suppression" laws, 111–112
voters, reaching out to, 128–136

W

Wallace, George, 96
Wannabe Kings. *See also* HCPs
(high-conflict personalities)
behaviors, 21
characteristics, 127–128
concept, 15
diagram, 16
"I alone can fix it," 50, 55
keeping up with, 159–160
shifting sides, 24
skills, 30
warning signs, 118, 141
Watergate scandal, 99–101
WEB Method, 142–145
words. *See also* blaming words
of caution, 146–147
noticing usage, 142–145
WWI (World War I), 61

Y

Yeltsin, Boris, 77–78
Yugoslav Wars, 1990s, 5–6

Z

Zedong, Mao. *See* Mao Zedong

ABOUT THE AUTHOR

 BILL EDDY is a lawyer, therapist, mediator, and co-founder and Training Director of the High Conflict Institute. He obtained his law degree from the University of San Diego, a master's degree of social work from San Diego State University, and a psychology degree from Case Western Reserve University. He has taught at the University of San Diego School of Law and the National Judicial College. Eddy currently provides training to professionals worldwide on the subject of managing high-conflict personalities and is a part-time faculty member at the Straus Institute for Dispute Resolution at Pepperdine University School of Law and at Monash University Law Chambers. He lives in California.

For more information and resources, visit

www.HighConflictInstitute.com

www.NewWays4Families.com

Dear reader,

Thank you for picking up this book and welcome to the worldwide BK community! You're joining a special group of people who have come together to create positive change in their lives, organizations, and communities.

What's BK all about?

Our mission is to connect people and ideas to create a world that works for all.

Why? Our communities, organizations, and lives get bogged down by old paradigms of self-interest, exclusion, hierarchy, and privilege. But we believe that can change. That's why we seek the leading experts on these challenges—and share their actionable ideas with you.

A welcome gift

To help you get started, we'd like to offer you a **free copy** of one of our bestselling ebooks:

www.bkconnection.com/welcome

When you claim your **free ebook**, you'll also be subscribed to our blog.

Our freshest insights

Access the best new tools and ideas for leaders at all levels on our blog at ideas.bkconnection.com.

Sincerely,

Your friends at Berrett-Koehler

Certified

Corporation